Melodies
Under The Palms

MEMORIES FROM THE IRAQ I USED TO KNOW

SALMA AJO, PH.D

authorHOUSE

AuthorHouse™
1663 Liberty Drive
Bloomington, IN 47403
www.authorhouse.com
Phone: 1 (800) 839-8640

Published by AuthorHouse   11/18/2015

ISBN: 978-1-4969-6662-9 (sc)
ISBN: 978-1-4969-6661-2 (hc)
ISBN: 978-1-4969-6660-5 (e)

Library of Congress Control Number: 2015903967

Print information available on the last page.

This book is printed on acid-free paper.

Warda LLC, Corporation.

Book Review

Dr. Salma Marougy Ajo, author of the recently released book *Melodies Under The Palms*, is the founder of Action Net Psychological Services, specializing in the treatment of alcohol and drug dependence. She was a Board Member of the Michigan Red Cross for over 10 years, and served on the Board of the Arab and Chaldean American Advisory Commission by appointment from Governor Jennifer Granholm. Dr. Ajo currently has a private practice in Farmington Hills, MI and treats clients with various types of addictions. This book was many years in the making, and Dr. Ajo discusses the motivations that contributed to it.

When asked about the inspiration to write this book, I often think back to my days as a graduate student. My thesis and dissertation work were filled with personal experiences related to the topics at hand. Colleagues often suggested a book to be something I should strongly consider writing in the near future, particularly one based on my background and life experience. The thought of writing this book was always there, I was just waiting for something to get me started. That something would be the Iraqi invasion of 2003. As an individual who grew up in Iraq, I was devastated to see the state of my homeland, and feared everything I knew and experienced would be gone forever. I often dreamt of taking my children back to Iraq, however, that seemed unlikely to ever happen.

The main objective of this book is to introduce the Iraq I used to know, and bring about a different perspective to a country that has been so harshly portrayed by the media. The reader will be taken back to a time where Iraq was filled with culture and diversity, and experience what it was like to grow up in the region of the Fertile Crescent. The true beauty of such a wonderful country will be brought to light and its vast history will leave readers in awe.

It is my hope that this book will raise a new level of awareness and bring about feelings toward a culture that seems all but gone forever. Although the Iraq I used to know is longer such, my memories will make sure that it stays with us for eternity. I am pleased to share my personal experiences and feel readers from all backgrounds will enjoy them.

Dedication

I would like to dedicate this book to my family who showered me with their love, blessings and support.

With all my love to my husband Ramzi Ajo, for your never-ending love, support, and patience during the hours I put into this book enforced what I already knew; your confidence in me! Thank you for taking over at home and giving me the opportunity to accomplish all of my educational goals. Completing this book is a tribute to everything we stand for.

To my children: Faris, his wife Asil and their amazing children Christian and Grace. My son Mahir for always being there for me. My youngest son Ramzi Jr and his wife Shennel, who recently welcomed their beautiful daughter Hailey Rose into the world. You are all are a constant reminder of the beauty and joy of childhood and growth. May we continue to grow in our relationships!

To my parents (may God bless their souls) who provided me with the best gift of healthy childhood and allowed me to grow to be the person I am today.

I also owe a great deal of thanks to many of my friends who have supported and encouraged me throughout the years of writing this book. Thank you for the confidence you instilled in me.

Finally, and most importantly, I would like to thank all the American Soldiers for their service to this wonderful country of ours during the war on Iraq. My heart also goes out to the innocent Iraqis who suffered unbelievably during the invasions bombings unleashed upon them. May God bless them and their families.

Introduction

Two major issues motivated me to write this book. (1) I felt overwhelmed with some speakers, politicians and journalists who introduce themselves as specialists in the Middle-East affairs with minimal knowledge after a short visit to these countries especially Iraq and they believe that they have the expertise to make decisions about these countries. I have the truth, knowledge, and the experience living in the Middle East, not only living in Iraq and visited most of the Arab countries such as Kuwait Lebanon, Syria, Jordan, Palestine, Egypt and Morocco. We visited almost every one of them as I was growing up, plus I identify and understand the different dialogues spoken in every Middle Eastern country. As you will be introduced to me through this novel you will find interesting and an eye-opener to my experiences growing up in Iraq, the neighboring countries and the discovery of my childhood and how I was exposed to for instance to speaking, reading and writing multiple languages.

So, I decided to write about the Iraq I used to know before the 70's, the Iraq I knew before we moved to the United States which is not the same Iraq I knew then. Growing up with loving family and most important it was a safe environment and children were innocent. It was a true example of "it takes a village to raise a child". So I decided to put my experiences into action, the experiences and challenges from my childhood toward my adulthood and to the present time. I believe that my unique upbringing and the courage to accept the changes that I was faced with is an example of growth and resilience to continue to be grounded with my strong upbringing values, looking at life in a logical way, understanding my own culture and trying to continue to be the person that I wanted to be and fulfill my dreams.

My journey was not a smooth there were some bumpy roads along the new path however, with faith, courage and commitment guided us in the right path that we decided to take and we were willing to overcome all obstacles. I do not regret the change that we devoted for our dreams to come true. Our strengths were we were both knowledgeable with the English Language, we were young and able to adapt to the new situation and bounce back and finally we were positive within our acceptance to our new life.

Moreover, for years I knew deep within my heart I am missing something I have not seen in Michigan. Until one day we were visiting San Diego, California and I saw a flowering plant that I recognized with a strong fragrance took me years back to my childhood, I did not know the name of the flower. So we visited a nursery to search and I found it and the tag labeled it as Arabian Jasmine. At this point my childhood memories guided me to write a book for my children and grand children and all the Iraqi children who will never have the chance to see the Iraq with the memories that they will never be able to experience of growing with **the Iraq I used to know**.

Chapter 1

Early experiences of Basra

Information is pretty thin stuff unless mixed with experience.
~Clarence Day- The Crow's Nest~

It is an early June at the crack of dawn in Basra. A cool breeze brushes lightly against my face. I am four years old. I pull the cover tightly and try to sleep more and enjoy the morning cool weather as I lie on the flat roof and I want to make-up for the lost sleep of the night before because my grandmother was telling us old stories while she was baby sitting for us.

All homes in Iraq use the flat roofs to sleep on in the summer because it is cooler than indoors. Our roof and my grand parents' roof were connected through a storage room and we could go back and forth to each other's house. After my grandmother makes sure that everyone is asleep she will go to her own bed on the roof over the house. Before the sun is up, singing birds wake us. And they keep on singing waking up the late sleepers. Usually I would stay asleep the longest since my bed was in an area that was hit with the sun last. Then I would sleep until the sun is up and the air became warm. Then my sleep is interrupted and I would go downstairs for breakfast.

My mother would have prepared breakfast for us as soon as we wake up in the morning. Traditional breakfast consisted of freshly baked bread from the neighborhood bakery, Khubus was a large round flat bread baked in tanoor a flat deep open grill. The process of the other bread called Samoon needs a different bakery called firin, which is a flat open grill. For breakfast khubuz or Samoon were baked fresh daily and delivered to the home early in the morning. Every family kitchen had dibis (date molasses) and homemade jams made with seasonal fruits served with Gamer (buffalo clotted cream).

Gamer is made out of the cream on the top of unpasteurized milk delivered by the milk woman who raises water buffalo and sells the milk. Sometimes she sells ready made Gamer, butter and cheese made from water buffalo milk. My mother would boil the milk and keep it in the refrigerator over night and the next day. It would form a thick layer of about one inch of cream on the top.

The next morning my mom would skim the cream that forms on the top of the milk and serve it for breakfast with home made jam from the fruit of the season and debis (dates syrup) served with the khubuz and samoon fresh from the neighborhood bakery. It was the best breakfast with Ceylon sweet tea and hot milk added. In addition to the traditional breakfast on special days my mother would make French toast that she learned from the English women she had met through my father's business associates.

We some times had home made Gamer (similar to Devonshire Cream) and seasonal jam/debis for breakfast. Food was purchased fresh and bought on a daily basis. Lamb and chicken are bought on the day it is going to be cooked. The Iraqi cuisine is the healthiest food you can imagine and we learned to eat in moderation even with our favorite food. It was expected to eat at home for all daily meals and mothers were expected to have a hot meal fresh cooked on the table where the family sat and enjoyed lunch, the main meal together.

Restaurants were available in Iraq, for people who came to town or single men with no one to cook for them. Seasonal fruits and vegetables were available for each season; winter vegetables were different from the summer ones. It was expected to have fresh food since canned or frozen foods were unheard of at that time.

Iraqi traditional cuisine goes back to the Mesopotamian era and was developed from ancient times in Chaldea, Sumer, Akkad, Babylonia and Assyria. It is considered the oldest cuisine. The food has been enhanced with different spices that were introduced to the country when Baghdad/Iraq was invaded by several nations. The location and the richness of the cuisine's resources became the center of the Abbasid Caliphate during the Islamic Golden Age while Europe was in the dark ages.

Muslims and other scholars from many parts of the world came to visit, live and study in Iraq, which gave the Iraqi cuisine new flavor for its food. This is most commonly seen in the superior use of different spices (e.g. saffron, cardamom and curry used by Iraqi cuisine in comparison to other Arab cuisines.)

Iraqi cuisine has been influenced by all the neighboring countries and has much in common with, Persian, Turkish, and Indian cuisines. With the Ottoman control Iraq and consequent influences of Turkish cuisine history, the Iraqi cuisine has been deeply influenced not only by its fertile land between the two rivers, Euphrates and Tigris, by neighboring countries. National dishes reflect all these influences.

I am still astonished today when I think back at all the changes I have witnessed in my lifetime, remembering also the stories that I had heard from my grandmother and my aunts. As a child I was born and raised in Basra, south of Iraq, the only port after the Arabian Gulf

I am the second oldest child of five siblings; three girls and two brothers. My mother had a girl after me who died as an infant when she was diagnosed with malaria. Basra was surrounded by rivers, canals and wetlands, encouraged mosquitoes and sometimes caused a common epidemic, malaria disease for Basra's residents.

I was born and lived next door to my grand parents from my mother's side. My family was a traditional Chaldean/Catholic family where dad worked and mother was a stay –at-home mom. She made most the decisions at home, including discipline. My mother was the second oldest daughter, who was the first to get married and that was against the norms in the Iraqi culture at the time. Normally, the older daughter gets married first.

My mom had four sisters and four brothers. It seemed to me then that I had several mothers including my grandmother and aunts who took care of us. When my grandmother cooked our favorite food, we were always welcome to go next door to eat with them.

I lived as I grew up, a simple life with love and affection, where children were treated as children, "to be seen and not to be heard." There was a lot of discipline at home, and equally the same at school. The rules were alike. We lived accurately, they old saying that, "It takes a village to raise a child". That was how I felt then and now. Girls learned at early age to act like young ladies and the same applied to the boys who were to behave like young gentlemen. Children respected and listened to their elders and adults respectfully took care of the young children.

I remember my grandmother's stories when she would put us to sleep as our parents went out for the evening. Her voice grew up and down as she told the stories as we were falling asleep. Quietly, she would leave for her own bed next door on the flat roof with a brick wall that divided the two homes and a small room that was used to connect the two homes. This also used as access/ divider and a door to get in their house, into ours. My memory of my grandmother is a big part of my childhood.

One of my grandmother's stories was about how parents were strict with their daughters especially at the time, when a girl was engaged: she was not allowed to go out with her fiancé alone. Always family members had to accompany her. My grandmother told me a story about a couple who were engaged and the fiancé one day wanted to take his fiancé to the movies. Her father was upset and he responded to his daughter's fiancé that he had no daughter to go to the movies and cancelled the engagement. My grand- mother stated that the couple finally did get married two years later. Friends intervened to resolve the conflict influencing the father to let the couple marry.

Our grand father loved us and cuddled us, giving us lots of attention when we went to visit. When he was sitting by the radio and listening to the news, we knew that we had to be very quiet. One thing we learned from my aunts was that my grandfather never hugged them or even acknowledged them as children, held them or kissed them while they were growing up. But he was different with us, the grand children to whom he gave special attention.

I remember that my grand father was a very well known person in Basra. He was a manager of the Othman Bank and because Basra was small we knew our neighbors and almost everyone in the city. We learned to whisper when speaking in public because we did not want others to know our business. Most people knew each other by first name or the family name.

I was told that my grandparents from both sides were the survivors of the Turkish Armenian/Christian genocide in 1915. However, my grandfather from my father's side, after surviving the Turkish genocide heard along the way that there was a village in north of Iraq with mainly a Christian population which encouraged him and other members of his community to travel and find a home there and live there. He settled in Telkaif, a small village in the north where most of the Chaldeans came from. He eventually was married and fathered three sons.

My maternal grandparents used to work on the farm and my grandfather's sister who was not married lived with them to take care of the children. One day their parents were late at the field and it was getting dark. Their uncle, who was their mother's brother, went with other men from the village and found them dead. He brought them to his house and informed the police. He did not want the children to see what was going on. (My cousin gave all the information to me when I started investigating my father's background).

According to my cousin, since his father was the oldest, he knew what was going on within his family. Catered to his other brothers including my father, being the youngest his parent's death was not explained. My cousin continued to inform me that our grandparents from our grandmother's side of the family took care of the boys and gave them their family name to protect them from cruel people who might mention the past to them.

This was an immense tragedy for my father's family. My father and his two brothers were taken by their aunt and uncle away from the village and headed south to Basra. This was done to escape growing up in the same village, and hearing different stories about their parent's deaths.

My father's uncle had heard that the Brits (British) were in Basra and there were plenty of jobs for him since he needed to take care of these three children. He knew Basra was the best option for them all and his sister agreed to take care of the children since she was taking care of them already, when their parents went to work.

So they took the boys and relocated to Basra. They lived in Basra and the three boys' uncle became successful and well known in Basra. Once my father and his brothers became adults, each one of them chose different jobs in different cities, but still in Iraq. My father's aunt, who had raised him, chose to stay with him in Basra, even after he married my mother.

His aunt was like a mother to him. My dad's aunt stayed with us and she helped my mother with the cooking and taking care of us, especially bathing us and washing the clothes. My dad's oldest brother and his family lived in Baghdad and kept in touch with my parents until they left Iraq for England with their two sons. As for my father's middle brother, we never met him

Now, looking back to my dad's family history, I understand why my dad was so reserved and sensitive. He was a loving father but kept to himself. I wish I knew these things before he died in 1996, so that I could have reached out to him and find out how he felt growing without both of his parents. I believe he was given lots of love, but he wanted to give us what he was missed his parent's presence in his life.

My father enjoyed a great deal of freedom and affluence in Basra during the 1940s and 50's, working with the British Company in Basra. Christian Iraqis emulated the Brits, dressing in the latest European fashions, speaking in English accents, even giving their children British names. My father Alexander spoke English beautifully with a British accent, which came in handy during the years when he worked for Andrew Weir at the British Date Processing Company as a quality assurance officer.

My mother and father lived a good life, and were respected by relatives and friends. They started their first home in Basra that was built in a traditional, oriental style, composed of two floors with a large, open-square courtyard in the middle. The bedrooms and the living area were at the ground floor, by the kitchen. On the second floor, overlooking the courtyard was the flat roof where we enjoyed sleeping on hot summer nights.

For leisure, adults loved to take boat rides on the Shat-Al-Arab River. They would stop at a little island where they were served fresh fish grilled inside a pit filled with wood sticks from fruit trees. Grilled Masquef is a famous grilled fish made on a bed of wood fire. Masquef is a traditional Iraqi dish that can be traced to thousand of years ago when Iraq was called Mesopotamia during the Chaldean and Assyrian rules.

My parents took advantage of the accessibility for leisure taking a relaxing boat ride during the evenings with a full moon on the calm and peaceful waters of shat-Al-Arab River, while listening to low music that added enjoyable and pleasant moments.

One of the great things around our house was my father being a provider for us. He was very generous and respected by everyone. My father gave us all the love and often gifts. Since, he was employed by a British Company, he adopted their cultural traditions and social as we were introduced to canned foods, visited the British specialized grocery stores and brought home items were not available to other families such as treats and gourmet canned food.

My father had a good job working as a Supervisor/Quality Assurance Inspector at the Basra Date Company (an English Base Company called Andrew Weir). During the (fall) autumn season, the date processing season starts. I remember my dad would spend days and nights at the company since they worked 24 hours around the clock to maintain the dates' freshness. My mom would take us to visit dad when he stayed days at work and we would go around observing the process of packing boxes that were ready to be shipped out of the country.

When the date season approached, we were the first ones to taste the dates before they were shipped. My father made sure to bring a big load to the house for our use and to ship some to relatives and friends in Basra and Baghdad. He had prepared the nuts earlier he bought almonds and walnuts for stuffing.

My tongue burns from the memory and sweet taste of Burhi dates stuffed with almonds and walnuts, which my father would bring in 50 pounds metal containers to save for winter. He also used to send them to Baghdad to his brother and relatives, and distribute them to friends and relatives, in Basra. Every one enjoyed our dates, knowing that my dad would bring home the best quality of dates.

Notice in the picture of my parents leaving the church on their wedding day, the decoration with the palms in the background that are used for good luck.

My father thought about everything and wanted to make things perfect and took pride in doing the best for us. He loved my mother and was proud of her. He wanted my mother to master the English language. He hired a tutor that came to the house to teach my mother how to speak English in order to be able to socialize with the British women. My mother, however, never mastered the English language, but managed to communicate and understand more than she spoke

Basra had the most palm trees in Iraq that produced dates. Iraq's dates are the second largest exports after oil. Most of these date palm farms in Basra were located on the west side of Shat El Arab which is about over a 100- mile long river formed by the joining of two main Iraqi rivers, the Tigers and Euphrates. These rivers stream towards the south where they merge together and form the Shat-El-Arab River that empties into the Persian Gulf. That's what makes Basra and Shat Al Arab unique. The farmers appreciated my father doing business with them because he was fair to them when he received most of their yearly crop. The managers loved his style of doing business with the farmers.

In return, my family was invited by several farm owners to their farms on a yearly basis to show their appreciation for their business relationship and for my dad to continue working with each of them. My dad knew exactly how to work with the farmers and keep them happy at the end of the season. This friendship was typical of Basrawi's culture. Most people who live in Basra are famous for their generous hospitality and opening their homes for friends, business colleagues, and even strangers.

During that time, the only way to cross Shat-El-Arab was by boats. I remember that when my dad worked in the Date Processing Company we were invited every spring. to the palm tree farms by the farm owners. My parents used to invite family and friends to join us in a lavish meal prepared by the family who owned the farms. This was their way of showing respect for my parents and expressing appreciating for their cordial business relationship.

The farmers used to send us 2-4 of their own motorboats to pick us up to cross the river to their farms. The trip took about 20 minutes one way. Upon our arrival at the family farm, the owners would be waiting by the boat dock with the whole family, including their wives and children. As a cultural hospitality tradition, the host would slaughter a lamb as we landed as a sign of joyful celebration and welcome us to their home.

In other cultures, children cannot witness killing an animal. But in the Iraqi culture since we were children, we grew up experiencing these events as celebrations. It was customary that on several occasions, such as Baptism, First Holy Communion, weddings and getting out of the hospital after a major surgery, always to sacrifice a lamb. Sometimes the lamb was sent to the orphanage. This tradition was practiced by all religions (Christianity, Judaism and Islam).

Culturally, on these occasions killing at least one lamb is a sign of respect and honor, and a way of welcoming my parents and their friends. On this occasion, killing a lamb was a sacrifice as a sign to thank God. The farms were beautiful; besides the palms there were every fruit, and many delicate flowers you could imagine growing under the palm trees to protected from the summer heat of the sun and enjoying the shaded areas.

After we were guided to the sitting area that was prepared for us, and the host made sure that everyone was comfortable, the women disappeared to prepare the lamb with the special spices. Later, they would grill the lamb with burning dry wood from fruit trees for us they would include all kinds of delicious Iraqi cuisine that they had prepared for us. Men and women were all busy entertaining and preparing the food.

Gondolas are a narrow boat with a curve at the ends. They use paddles and controlled by a long pole. When riding on the gondolas, we could enjoy the beauty of the farms. We usually stayed to watch the sundown and the farmers would take us and our guests back to cross Shat al Arab where the cars were parked to go home.

The farmer's family would make us comfortable. Their children and their nanny would take us around to show us the fields and play games that had been prepared for us earlier. They also would take us to visit their vegetable and fruit gardens. Then they gave us permission to cut the ripped fresh fruit and vegetables as the nanny pointed out the ripe ones. For me, that was the best part of the picnic. I always enjoyed cutting the ripped fruits and vegetables and eating them right away. They were grown without chemicals.

Those annual events continued for years until *Andrew Weir-The British Date Processing Company was nationalized by the Iraqi government.* 1n 1956. It took them a few years to re-structure the new Company and rehire new employees. My dad did not go back to work with the new management after being used to the British management, he knew it wouldn't be the same. He ended up opening his own business and was not successful, since he was honest and hated to overcharge people. After

I was married and moved to Baghdad, my dad found a job in Kuwait and came home only on weekends.

Al-Zubayr is a town in southeastern Iraq. This historical town to the Muslim community where you can still see the remains of the mosque dedicated to the memory of the Prophet Muhammad who was killed in a the Battle in this city.

Locations in the desert between Basra and Zubair were very attractive, open and private sheltered areas where the British had planted evergreen trees in the desert to use for the Christmas season. Basra's weather is hot and humid in the summer, cold and rainy in the winter. Basra has a typical four seasons weather that makes this area great location for picnics. Spring was the best season where to enjoy these outings. We enjoyed these outings when the weather is pleasant and comfortable.

My family, cousins, friends and I with the children in the Evergreen Trees called Ethel (1948). My family, relatives and friends used to make arrangements ahead of time to go out for picnics in this area in the outskirts of Zubair where they would pick a good shaded area to camp in. Everyone met at a place called Ethel. The area describes a tree or bush that retains its foliage throughout the year (evergreen area in Arabic). Besides the evergreen trees, visitors to this area enjoyed the countryside scenery setting, a breathtaking view with layers of colorful flowers everywhere covering the ground like a carpet.

The children played around the trees and the men played cards and socialized and the women socialized while preparing the food and watching their own children. Our aunts always watched our cousins and us.

Some of the women would take the opportunity to learn how to drive a car or a bike, other young boys and girls would play soccer ball or tennis. The mothers spent most of the time preparing to serve the food, and others prepared to barbeque lamb chunks pieces that had been marinated. Others cooked the chicken and put together the vegetables and fruits. On these occasions men and married women would drink beer and the rest would drink soda. Music and dancing were always part of these outings.

These were some of the happy days during my childhood as I was growing up in Basra/Iraq I will leave these memories behind to my children and grandchildren and all the children of the Iraqi and Chaldean descent that I know. They will never be able to see what I experienced during the mid-forties to the end of mid-sixties before we left (or before we had to leave) Iraq.

I am proud that I had kept journaling my memories to keep thing fresh in my mind. This book is the products of my exposure to events and people in my past that. events that changed my philosophy and my outlook.

Khubuz (flat bread)   Samon

Home-made Gamar (similar to Devonshire Cream)
and seasonal jam/debis for breakfast

Packing Company
(Andrew Weir 1946)

My father, first one on the
right with colleges, friends
and farmers on a business trip
to the date farms (1948)

My dad with farmers
in the farm (1944)

My parents at the
date farm (1948)

My parent's wedding leaving the church. (1940)
Notice the decoration with the palms in the
background that are used for good luck.

Some family and friends as we arrived at the farm without the children (1947)

On of the boats that belong to the farmers with my cousins (1948)

Family members in the gondola

*This is an old picture of my grandfather and great
grandfather who is playing an old traditional Iraqi
musical instrument (Oud) with the farm owner on Shat Al Arab in 1940.*

*This picture will give the reader an idea of the
area with the evergreen trees. (1946)*

family, cousins, friends and I with the children in
the Evergreen Trees called Ethel (1948)

Chapter 2

Experience is not what happens to you,
It's what you do with what happens to you.
-Aldous Huxley

I saw the world differently and had the courage to risk everything to honor that vision. This is not my own creation, but what was certain is that I am sharing my personal reality of a true picture of Basra as I saw it and lived it all those years one third of my life before I left the country. When I talked to friends and colleagues about my life growing in Basra I heard compliments and I would hear "You have had a great and extraordinary life, you should write a book about your life story; This reflects the telling of my story and journey.

History of Basra

With a population of 1.3 million people, Basra is the second largest city in Iraq. Located on the Shatt Al-Arab River and close to the Persian Gulf, Basra is Iraq's primary port. There is along explanation and history behind it.

Basra continued to be an important trade center during the Ottoman and Persian occupation period, and was one of the provincial capitals in Iraq. Because it became a highly developed and sophisticated natural environment, Basra was the home to significant Iraqi nationalist opposition to the Ottoman ruling in the early 20th century.

Basra is the largest city in southern Iraq situated on the west bank of Shatt Al-Arab, about 50 km from the Arabian Gulf and 500 km from Baghdad. It is the main entrance and exit to the outside world by water. The main port of Iraq, Al-Basra had an international airport.

Basra also was connected by rail with Baghdad and the countries of Iran, Turkey and Germany. It is the terminal point for oil pipelines. Petroleum refineries were a major industry where oil was processed, developed and purified.

Basra is important in terms of Iraq's and Islam's history, and is surrounded by the largest plantation of date palms in the world. Those date palms trees were the backbone of Basra's industry after the oil. The canals that crisscross Basra has given a distinctive to its creature gave a distinctive character to Basra known as the **"Venice of the East"**. About 70 km north of Basra is the location of Qurna, (site of Adam and Eve tree's of the forbidden fruit) was known for this.

The Qurna is located at the fork of the Tigris and Euphrates. According to legend, it is the site of the **Garden of Eden.** The two great rivers, the Tigris and the Euphrates, pass through the country from north to south. The Tigris passes Baghdad and the Euphrates passes Syria and enters Iraq. The two rivers then meet at Qurna, and about a few Kilometers after it meets with the Shatt-Al-Arab, which runs through Basra in the south to pour into the Arabian Gulf.

Basra was a pluralistic, socially diverse city. Although most of population is Shiites, it also is the home to considerable communities of Sunnis (Arabs and Kurdish), Jews, Christians (primarily Chaldean, Assyrian, and Armenian) and the black minority (zinj). Basra's residents were proud that the city was highly diverse community and sophisticated, highly developed and cosmopolitan. The dean of Basra University said:

> *"People in Basra have always wanted to live in peace, accepting others regardless of their sectarian or religious identity. Christians live beside Muslims and Sunnis besides Shiite. At one point, we even had a large Jewish minority. We are used to living among such diversity. People have always been accustomed to living with foreigners and members of other faiths. Christians, Jews and Muslims in Basra were indeed open-minded"*

Basra's people were always known as laid back and peaceful compared to other Iraqis. Nevertheless, the old Basra (when wealthy people moves to the new Basra where new sub-divisions where built," was finally abandoned altogether on its transfer to the present site of the new Basra. The new Basra was situated as near to the Shatt-al-Arab as the level of ground would permit to avoid the danger of flooding. The city grew, and later followed the river port of Ashar became the main inlet and outlet for the nation's merchandise.

As Iraq's only port, is situated at the lower confluence of the Tigris and Euphrates Rivers,(and at the furthest practical point for the Trans-shipment of goods from the ocean going to more expensive inland transportation facilities. However, the City Margil was chosen as the most suitable site for the development of large wharves.

The modern state of Iraq was created in 1920, as part of a peace settlement following the war. The conquering allies seized and divided the Arab provinces of the former Ottoman Empire between them. Britain, had occupied the provinces of Basra and Baghdad for most of the war. Basra became the center from which Iraqi nationalists began to demand a measure of independence and self-government.

The Shatt al Arab is navigable and protected by maritime traffic for about 130 km. The Tigris and Euphrates Rivers have navigable sections for shallow-draft watercraft. The Port of Umm Qasr is situated south of Basra at the doorway of the Shat El Arabs and is the only seaport for direct deliveries into Iraq. This area was very busy with commercial boats moving in and out of the river to the gulf.

The region of Basra, the city of Sinbad, is, I would say, the most beautiful part of Iraq; outshining both the 'Persian miniature' scenery of the central Euphrates and the cool, majestic north. I was born and raised in Basra and I always preferred it to Baghdad. The whole area is luxurious with lavish, full of palm trees, gardens and canoes gliding on the mirror-surfaces of calm lagoons.

This is an area where you see countless birds and a variety of animals. An Island close to the riverbank bears his name. Sinbad's Island in Basra is famous for the Basrawi's picnic. In the spring when the weather is comfortable for the outdoors, families and friends gather together and spend the day in fun. Families young and old take their food and music where they dance, eat and drink while children play.

Some families would fish, clean the fish and cook it on the spot. Fish Masgouf is a famous grilled fish processing outdoors. At the same time families enjoyed the benefit of the fresh fish availability to grill at this island.

The river-edge parts of Basra are what most Basrawis dream of from abroad. The Ashar is the heart of the city; it is covered by bazaar and mosque at the end of the creek that link it by the river to old Basra.

On the other side of the bank you can take a canoe *(bellam* in Iraqi), a ferry or a motor-launch up and down the bustling river; or relax in one of the tea-houses that overhang the river on the corniche (river front) south the Ashar creek; or drink orange-soda and watch the ferry carrying people and trucks, bicycles and horses, handcarts and camels across the river. Being at that area is to meet friends and chat. On shore there were a few of the magnificent old Turkish mansions once used by British shipping firms or banks. Life was peaceful and people were laid back and enjoyed the serenity of the atmosphere.

From Ashar's low, blue-tiled mosque, motor boats splutter back and forth in small pale blue clouds of exhaust fumes. Passenger launches with crowded wooden roofs give the best view, pass and re-pass from one landing-stage to another; tugs drag long chains of iron barges to be loaded or emptied alongside the steamers in a flurry of clangs and clanks and reverberating shouts from foremen and stevedores. It is a lovely river; and it is alive.

Basra has been called the Venice of the East, but this is misleading and unfair. Of course, Basra contains nothing architecturally comparable to Venice. It does, however, have many canals and they add real enchantment to the scene.

The port is always over-full: ships of ten thousand or twelve thousand tons lie alongside the jetties opposite the handsome, domed Port Authority Building on the shore at Maaqal remains since 1930s such as the Shatt al Arab Hotel is just up the road. The port wharf cannot cope with the sea-traffic of modern Iraq, and lower down the river for several miles the steamers stand in line in mid-river, bows pointing upstream, equal distant from each other like ships in a naval review.

British artist, Donald Maxwell, who came here in the 1920s, and who had been unimpressed by Basra up till then, wrote ecstatically of 'palms and gardens on the right quoting. Does the citation begin with "...of palms...." or does it begin with

> *"A British artist.... Indicate somewhere (in parentheses at the end?) where this citation comes from. If the whole paragraph is a quotation, use 'quotes and double quotes after lake--.'" Then give the rand buildings of the town on the left, and boats approaching, dream-like in the sunset glow . . . For once,'-he added, 'we have something that can surpass in beauty anything that Venice can show . . . Hundreds of palms seem to be growing out of a lake."*

Ships from India to the Mediterranean the route followed two principal courses sailed to Basra, and the traveler would stay a few days to organize things, travel up the western bank of the Euphrates via Samawa, (Diwaniya) and Hilla, to Baghdad and Aleppo. Travel was by camel caravan was dangerous at that time. Safety was in numbers, and, with luck the traveler would reach Aleppo.

The Bazaar

As a child I remember around the 1950's the older parts of Ashar were still very attractive. The most enjoyable discussions with my aunts or my mother were about Ashar. The covered bazaars had a distinct character and were worth roaming through the souk. These variety stores were quite widespread with big shops, were well stocked with imported merchandise; the smell of spices, herbs and coffee was everywhere; there was an old-world atmosphere in that place. I understand that there have been many changes since I lived there but I miss those feelings. I wish that I had taken my children to see their history before the change.

Our best time during those days was when we went to the bazaar. Mothers are with their children shopped and enjoying looking for things to purchase. That was the place to meet other families and friends. You could spend hours strolling up and down the street having fun without buying anything.

As you strolled through the bazaar you would see cosmetic stores, pharmacies, Bata shoe store, lightning fixture stores, other independent shoe stores, several fabric stores, and bookstores. Walking toward the end of the bazaar you would reach the spice stores where vendors grind and mix the spices, as requested for different recipes. Past the spice venders you would find yourself around the goldsmith's stores.

Along the creek outside the bazaar, coffee houses could be seen in the more modern jumble of new Basra; street-sellers peddle little things; anything from torch batteries and tomatoes, to dancing toys and onion sandwiches. For tourists there are Arab headdresses, local silver bracelets, coffee pots, camel-saddles. The coffee houses were mostly for men who are playing the bag-amen seated on clean and bright and wooden benches covered with raffia mats.

In these coffee shops you didn't need to provide your own tobacco in those days. And the men you saw puffing clouds of smoke were not Janissaries (see Glossary of terms) but the merchants, taxi-drivers, tradesmen and workers of Basra. It was interesting to pass the time watching the different sorts of people who came to these coffee houses or the crowds sauntering back and forth before their entrances.

An English traveler, the Hon. George Keppel, passing through Basra on his way home from India in the early 1800s, described a scene not unlike what you can see today:

> *Throughout the bazaar, we observed numerous coffeehouses; they are spacious, unfurnished apartments, with benches of masonry round the walls, raised about three feet from the ground. On these are placed mats; at the bar are ranged numerous coffeepots, and pipes of different descriptions. It is customary for people to bring their own tobacco. These houses are principally filled by Janissaries, who were puffing clouds from their pipes in true Turkish taciturnity.'*

Homes in Old Basra

On both sides of the creek rows of great houses stood staring at each other from high, pointed windows and latticed *shenashils (Turkish style)*, the overhanging wooden structures in which the people of the house could sit and watch passers-by below as well as have a cool breeze in the summer evening heat. *The shenashil* built with iron rail supports were constructed after the arrival of the British in 1915.

Along the creek the French school/convent where I attended school with the French Dominican sisters is located in the old Basra. On our way to school we would pass these beautiful houses that made out of carved wood windows. As we began growing up, we then learned these were called Shenashil (Iraq has a lot of the Turkish and Persian influence and some words were mixed together with the Iraqi language that is being used today).

The houses are of yellow brick. Their windows are often protected from the appalling Basra heat by long, broad shutters held open by adjustable iron struts, a special feature of Basra architecture. Here were streets after streets of rich family homes. These houses were imprinted in my memories for me to retain since we passed these houses every day from and to school. Memories take me back to Basra.

Why is Basra significant?

Basra is a significant city because of the oil, experts Shiite militias are fighting over that crown in the jewel," Basra, until recently one of Iraq's safest cities, is important to the central government in Baghdad not only because the city's oil fields provide around 90 percent of Iraq's budgetary revenue but also because it is Iraq's major outlet to the Persian Gulf.

Iraq's Eternal Plant (Palm Trees)

The age-old date palm had already cast its shadow upon the **Garden of Eden,** when Adam and Eve revealed their first proof of human weakness. There is archaeological evidence that the ancient races of who lived in houses roofed with date palm ferns. The date palm is, therefore, often thought of as the most ancient tree in the world and is frequently referred to as the "Eternal Plant."

Basra is the home of the date palm is Iraq, **the Eternal Land of Sunshine.** The weather conditions are ideal for date growing, more than 80 percent of the world's supply of dates is grown at that time. The most valued tree is the date palm – the Nakhla (as it is called in Arabic). Tall trees, remarkable, beautiful, proud and tough but these trees required constant attention.

A fully-grown tree can endure decades of neglect. However, it requires a great deal of care to fully flourish and bear fruit-- much like Iraq. The tree is so important that to harm it is almost unforgivable. During the early Islamic military campaigns, a well-known guideline by a leader to his troops going off to far away lands was the following: "Do not kill a woman, a child or an old man. Do not cut a tree."

The natural fields were perfect for growing the date palms. Unless special provisions are made to accumulate and divert the surface water, rainfall has little importance in supplying the palm with its daily water requirements. In the majority of cases the cultivated date palm, therefore, has to be irrigated, either from rivers, streams, or wells.

Natural forces, such as gravity, when rivers originate uphill and their waters can be diverted into the date gardens, by artesian wells, or by tidal irrigation (tidal current: a horizontal displacement of ocean water under the gravitational influence of Sun and Moon, causing the water to pile up against the coast at high tide and move outward at low tide.) That helped the Basra area is renowned for its date crop of outstanding quality.

Beside the oil fields for the date palm farms that our family always visited every year, is a large, partially-tended expanse of nebek trees and palm groves, the last bearing clusters of un-ripened dates high with their spiky green leaves. Intermingled among weeds and foot-high grasses are small vegetable plots—cucumbers, okra, red pepper, figs and bamber—an Indian fruit about the size of a cherry tomato. (It is delicious when pickled.)

Most of these farms have been in the same family for centuries, as the farm owners that we visited on yearly basis informed us. Along the banks of the canals, are still green waters streaked with the copper glow of sunset.

"I can say that I am a real Iraqi," and I say it with pride. Although I became American by choice, I will always have a special place in my heart for Iraq where I lived a third of my life. It was a great experience and wish I could have visited Iraq before the invasion. Living in Iraq was such a wonderful experience. I wish I could share adequately my memories and feelings for this country and describe the peace that we once knew. How I wish I could have taken my children and my grandchildren to see Iraq before everything changed.

Some of my memories, and feelings for the nature and resources and peace that once this country had tranquility and harmony. I wished I had the chance to take my children and my grand children to see Iraq before the changes.

I know that I was a third generation living in Basra. My parents and my grandparents complained about my generation and talked about the good old. However, understand what "the good old days really were— for my generation.

I believe my generation was the last one to have that great significance meaning to life I once had the good fortune to live in the great country called Iraq. With pride, I say that as native a daughter of Basra—not only did my family reside in the city for several decades, but three to four generations were well known to the other Basrawi's who lived in the westernized city of Basra.

Every year, an expert has to go up each tree at least 4 times. The lowest row of drying leaves have to be removed, with the base cut in such a way to provide a foot hold for the climber. In April it has to be pollinated. In August, the dangling fruit bunches have to positioned so as to be supported by leaf stems or the main trunk. In September or October, the dates are harvested.

Iraq's southern port city of Basra, once the heart of trade and tourism, was also known for being the birthplace of Sinbad the Sailor. My memories take me back when Basra was a regional trade hub and its casinos, palm-dotted parks and mild weather made it a playground for wealthy Gulf Arabs, many of them from Kuwait to visit and shop the best meats from the cattle in southern Iraq that were slaughtered on a daily basis.

In the 1950s to early 1970 Basra evolved into a tourist destination with many Kuwaitis crossing the border in search of good times. Gulf Arabs and Kuwaitis visited Basra every weekend to enjoy the nightlife and great food especially the alcohol since alcohol is forbidden in Kuwait.

Yes, you see, Basra was once like that. It is, you know, a port city. The city was open to different cultures influenced from around the world—Asia, Europe, Africa, America as well as the countries of the east such as the gulf India and china and every country in between.

In the 50s, 60s, 70s, — when we walked through the Corniche waterfront the street was a river walk. On one side were bars and casinos and nightclubs, and on the other side across the river you would see thousands and thousands of palm trees reaching to the sky.

The Basra International Airport provided daily flights as well as transit flights that stopped in Basra for trips to be able to re-fuelling. The airport had a large hotel to accommodate al passengers from all counties and also to re-fuel the planes that stops.

The airport provided lodging for visitors with a very large indoor and outdoor restaurant for people to spend evenings. It had also an Olympic swimming pool and another smaller cafeteria. When we had nothing to do, we went to the airport for ice cream and watched the planes leave and land every ten minutes. Many times we would see friends or relatives travelling in and out of Basra. These memories I truly treasure, I miss the past that I knew.

Arabian Jasmine

There were Europeans, Indians sailors with their uniform as well as Basra natives. People gambled, drank Arak, had sex and prayed. They may have sinned, but they did it indoors, with the result that "Allah forgave them." The other side of town there were all the municipality buildings and homes of the government officials, their fences covered with Arabian Jasmine vines. The aroma of the flower would stay with you for days.

These white fragrant flowers with pink buds in the spring grow fast and open with double five petals. They are also referred as Winter Jasmine or its hardiness (about 15 degree F). In order to protect these flowers from the harsh southwestern sun when planted outdoors it is best to put them next to a wall that offers both protection and support. That is why Arabian Jasmine does best in Basra with its hot weather in summer, humidity and mild winter.

Arabian Jasmine does well outdoors, though it thrives outside because of the weather and the humidity. Basra's weather is very close to the weather in San Diego. Its flowers are large and multi-layers, with round petals, shaped like small white roses.

What I look forward to someday, if we are lucky enough during our life, is when to travel to Iraq has peace and freedom. I will be able to take my children or they will take their own children to visit the country for them to see where we came from. I wish that Iraq could be a peaceful place where my family can visit and appreciate where they came I wish I could experience normal life there again. At this time as Iraqi Americans, we visit other Middle-Eastern countries but not our own Iraq, which I have never visited since we left in 1971.

My cousin and I in the
boat at Shat El Arab

The family in a Gondola

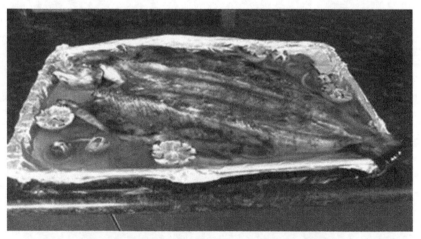

From my kitchen - Fish Masgouf (Grilled)

(I am in front) 1949 -My sisters with my cousins. At
the right side are the natural irrigation swales.

Arabian Jasmine with white flower on my deck

Chapter 3

Growing up in Basra

Memory is a way of holding onto the things you love,
and the things you are, the things you never want to lose.
~From the television show The Wonder Years~

It is October 31, a beautiful fall day and it is my 5th birthday. The skies are clear blue and the weather just started to change from the heat and humidity of the summer to a cooler fall breeze.

Basra has truly four seasons. I am excited since I have a birthday party planned for me after school. Since I am in Kindergarten, the bus will pick me up in the afternoon. While I am waiting for the bus my mother is preparing for my birthday party decorating the cake for my birthday. Mom entertained a lot since my dad was one of the managers in his company. Jabar was the pastry specialist who came to the house to help my mom to make the desserts, cakes and pastries.

Jabar, the Pastry Specialist was a stocky middle-aged man who went to homes where they can afford his services to help with special occasions. Our house was one of his best customers since my parents entertained a lot of family and friends, as well as business personnel who worked with my father. So my mom learned a lot from Jabar and used his skills for our birthday cakes until she started to make them herself and decorated them in professional ways. It seemed that I took after her when I was growing up.

While my mother was busy, my older sister and I were playing on the terrace (flat roof). There was a railing in the middle where you could see the lower level sun fresh air and light came into the house through the courtyard.

We were playing and going up and down the stairs when my naughty sister pushed me down the stairs and I fell on my head where my forehead started bleeding. My mother was a knowledgeable and did not panic. There is a big difference knowledgeable person who did not panic. Right away she wrapped my head with a bandage and asked me to lie down and rest for the afternoon.

Next, I heard my mother telling the bus driver that I would not be able to go to school that day. This was the second time to my recollection that my older sister was just naughty. It was obvious that my sister was jealous since I was the baby sister and my aunts favored me over her.

I have memories of my childhood, a childhood I treasure because I believe that a healthy childhood is the most important seed for an adult. We lived a block from the main Chaldean church, and we could hear church bells ring at least twice a day—and sometimes for weddings—or a death. This area was called the Kandaq since there was a canal at the end of the street.

We visited the church several times a week and my grandfather was a head of the deacons; my mother and aunts were involved in the Society of the Ladies of Charity. When we attended church we had to be on our best behavior since we were well known and we were instructed to behave like young ladies. At early age, we learned good ethics and proper etiquette. Because my mother was well known for her talent and creativity, other mothers commented about our outfits.

According to my aunts, I was told that people used to borrow our outfits to try to imitate the design. My grandfather, the Othman bank Manager, encouraged this. He ordered fashion magazines and catalogues directly from France for my mother. We were not the only ones my mom made clothes for. She used to work with the sewing machine all day to make things for my aunts and cousins and anyone that asked for a favor.

I grew up with parents who encouraged education, and identified with my mother. Who taught me other skills besides the education she knew I would learn in my mother would keep me busy all summer working on needlepoint and embroidery for bed sheets and pillow cases that she had traced and gave me to work on them.

I became so famous in the neighborhood that neighbors would borrow me to teach their children needlepoint work that I had mastered. My older sister was much less competent, so my mom gave up on her.

My younger sister too fragile, she was sick after her birth where she has pneumonia, and was weak to get involved with us the children. I felt I was robbed of my childhood, but at the same time I feel that my circumstances benefitted me because I gained a passion of creativity for craft, needlepoint, knitting and much more.

For several summers, my mother kept me busy. My older sister was not interested in work and would sit with other girls and young women to talk and visit. My younger sister was too young to do anything.

My Great Aunt Mary

Aunt Mary was my mother's aunt. She was the only sister to my grandmother. Aunt Mary lived with my grandmother and she spoiled us rotten. Aunt Mary had been educated in India. She came back speaking only English since she had attended school in Calcutta where her step-father-- who was legally blind—had taken her and her sister --,my grandmother-who was pregnant with my mother--With my great grand father's four-year old son with them, they all sailed to Calcutta in 1924.

The trip took 30 days. They enrolled my great-aunt in a boarding school. By that time my grandmother was very uncomfortable but did not want to give birth on a ship if they attempted to return.. So they decided to stay in Calcutta until my grandmother had the baby.

On December 31, 1924, my mother was born in Calcutta, India. Her grandfather waited for the new mother to get well before she attempted to travel back to Basra. Finally, my grandmother, the baby, her brother returned to Basra. Years passed and finally my aunt Mary came back from India. She spoke only English. Aunt Mary was hired right away at the port administration dealing with the foreigners. She had a side job/ tutored/teaching the English Language to children on the side.

Because she was a little heavy, she enjoyed walking and we would love going with her for a walk to the Corniche along the Shat-Al-Arab. I enjoyed seeing the sailors that Aunt Mary would stop to talk with, and

I would fantasize to be a grown girl and to learn how to communicate with the sailors who traveled from one country to another. I always had a special affection in my heart for sailors.

Aunt Mary was well respected by adults and loved by children. She had a special character that drew others to love her. I loved my family. Each one had a distinctive character-- my uncles, my aunts, my grand parents, and especially my parents. Much of this book is about growing up among a very well known family in the Iraqi city of Basra. We were proud of our family and we tried to be just like our elders—our role models in everything.

My mother and father lived a good life, and enjoyed special advantages. For example, their house in Basra was built in the traditional, eastern style, composed of two floors with a large, open-square courtyard in the middle. The house had bedrooms and main bathroom, kitchen, dining room, living room and a large hallway at the entrance. The bedrooms were on the second floor, overlooking the courtyard, though we enjoyed sleeping on the roof on hot summer nights.

Summer was great with the heat. I did not like winter. It was too cold. My dad would have a gas heater in every room and it was shut off at night. Sleeping in bed was cold in winter and my mother would put a hot water bottle (a plastic rectangle flat bottle especially for hot water that every home has for each individual that lives in the house to warm the bed until we went to sleep. The next morning the room is cold and getting out of the worm bed into a cold room was a challenge for us kids. There was no central heat

The family enjoyed the boat rides on the Shat-Al-Arab River. They would stop at a little island where they were served fresh charcoal-grilled Masguef, a fish similar to white fish that can grow as long as two feet in length. My mother always talked about the good old days and after she left, she wished to come back. She said that along with her parents they enjoyed a great deal of freedom and affluence in Iraq in the 1930s and '40s under the British, who had taken over the country from Turkey after World War I.

In gratitude, many of the more well to do Basra Christians emulated the British and French-- according to my grandfather, who spoke six languages-- dressing in the latest European fashions, speaking in a British English accent, even giving their children European names. My father spoke English beautifully, with a British accent, which came in handy during the years when he worked for the British Date Processing Company as a quality control officer.

I believe that my mother wanted to keep me away from my sister. So with my uncle and his wife, my aunt (my mother's sister), treated me as part of their family as if I had been adopted. I was always with them and expected to stay over at their house with their children who were close to my age. I enjoyed being with my cousins, and loved the special attention of my aunt and uncle. They treated me as their own daughters.

My uncle encouraged me to use the gymnastic bars that he had installed in his house on the side of the garden. I became an expert and adapted well like a Sponge with gymnastics. My uncle also taught me swimming. I was young like a sponge, wanting to learn everything that made my uncle happy, to have him teach me anything I was capable of learning.

It was a must for me to spend every weekend and the summer holidays with them until they left to Baghdad when I was ten years old. My uncle treated me as a princess. He was strict and much harder with his own children. When it came to the house rules, he did not apply them to me. His own children were to get fish oil every morning (kids hated it and had to study at designated times on a daily basis. They had chores each was responsible to complete. These rules were not applied to me. At the time, my mom went over my homework before I left the house.

My uncle worked with the English company (Basra Petroleum Company (BPC). He was given a home inside the Company's Executive compound that was fenced and guarded 24 hours a day. He had the same privileges working with the English as my father had working with the Dates Processing Company. My uncle earned more than my father since the BPC British/Basra Petroleum Company was very large.

My uncle's benefits were the same as his English Colleagues. He had access the swimming pools, private clubs and children's activities. My recollections to those memories: between my dad's British Date Packing Company British Petroleum Company associates and my uncle. The BPC introduced us to western social life at an early age and changed my outlook on life. My life was very different from that of others who grew in the country at the same period.

Traditional home with a court in the middle
(Picture from Encyclopedia of the Orient)

Gas heater (Aladdin Brand)

Chapter 4

Venice of the East (The Iraq I used to know)

"If you have not seen Iraq you have not seen the world"
John J. Donohue, S.J.
An American Priest at St. Joseph's University,
Beirut, Lebanon

All of us have stories of our childhood. My story is set against the backdrop of the final years of British presence in Iraq. To fully understand my story, it is important to understand the history of Iraq, the story of its citizens including the Christian/Chaldean and Jewish small communities and the subtle adjustments as well as dramatic transformations experienced by the residents of this growing metropolitan area and the nationals of the country called Iraq.

The Iraq I used to know

Basra, I believe that I was lucky to be born and raised in Basra, Iraq's second largest city and main seaport. Basra is situated 130km from the Gulf and 550km southeast of Baghdad. Modern Basra consists of three main areas:

Ashar, which is the old commercial centre, including the Corniche and the bazaars

Margil, which includes the port and modern residential areas

Basra, the old Basra was in the old residential area, where many beautiful, old- style houses were to be found. The Basra's Bazaar in the *Ashar* area was full of old houses with balconies leaning over into the narrow streets and beautiful wooden facades in the older style of Arab/ Turkish architecture. It was once contained a gold bazaar, selling fine pieces of gold jewelry, however I do not know whether this is still in existence at this time. When I lived in Basra during the 50's, 60's, and early seventies before I immigrated to the United States, Basra, was a beautiful city.

Spring was great with the scented smell like a bouquet or several flowers. We were able to trace the aroma of the Arabian Jasmine, the orange blossoms and the date blossoms. The fragrance would be hitting you from all sides when the breeze blows across our face. There is no other such experience and I will never experience that again anywhere in the world. That is why I feel fortunate to have lived in the beautiful and attractive Iraq. The country I grew up with. It is unique and close to my heart. As much as I describe the situation, the reader will never be able to imagine the beauty of nature in Basra.

Many young couples came to Basra to enjoy their honeymoon in the city during the 60's and 70'. The city was famous as a honeymoon destination. Newly married couples would wander along its graceful waterway - the Shatt al-Arab - and watch the tugboats and canoes drift past the droopy palm trees. These days, Basra has not quite recovered its old glory as Iraq's answer to the Riviera.

Basra is a City of Canals.

Because of its many cafes, a large red light district and practiced religious tolerance, Basra has been called Venice of the Middle East. The beauty stretches across the river where there are thousands of palm trees. Most of the date farms were located across the Shatt El Arab River and on the banks of the canals that were scattered in Basra City.

A Long History

The Zung referred to the Africans who were brought on ships from Africa and landed in Basra looking for jobs. I was not aware of the Africans' presence in Basra. I remember that my grandparents had a servant whose name was (Mouhee) and I thought he had dark skin. He was considered part of the family. When I was doing some research asking family and close friends from Basra, my mother mentioned that there was a special area in Basra when the Zunj lived as a community. My mom said that Mouhee was born when his mother made their living by washing clothes for my grandparents and later on as Mouhee was growing up in their house, he became their servant.

Now, as I write about Basra after 40 years plus perhaps that everything is getting mixed up in me. What is certain is that I am trying to paint an exquisite magical picture of Basra as I saw it and lived in it all of those years, a third of the years of my life until I left the country. On the other hand, because I know that my life is so interesting to others I decided to put my background down on paper.

I know that everything I am writing about Basra takes on a distinct meaning for me since I was young and sheltered in a Catholic school as well as at home. Am I in fact that child who spent her entire childhood living next door to her grandparents' house in Basra? Am I that young lady who got to know Basra street-by-street because of the size of the city and kept going by bus to school from the Khandaq to school at the old Basra. Sometimes Basra seems like a map with no lines or features. Sometimes Basra seems like a map with no lines or features and I have to draw them from my imagination.

My memories extend to some salty earth, with groves of date palms extending along its edges, and a wide river named Shutt al-Al-Arab. As for the rest, I recognize some areas by name: Umm al-Baroom, all of the different neighborhoods, the Corniche (river view), the churches, the bordellos, the taverns, the marketplaces, the cinemas. The beautiful white low winter clouds that passed over the tower of the Chaldean Church one short block from my house. Seemed to look like white cotton candy.

"Because, only he who travels discovers Basra City."

Now, as during all of these long years, I continue to remember Basra and my love and relationship to Basra, its neighborhoods and its buildings both public and private. The railway station, the port, and Sinbad's Island, the naval headquarters, the old Basra, the courthouse, al-Watan Street with its nightly festivities, with its nightclubs where all of the world's sailors would gather, in Mary's and Matilda's Bars and Sheena liquor store adjacent to the international store "Spinnys," that carried canned vegetables and fruits used by foreigners.

All of these years, I had Basra close to my heart; my ear has enjoyed the music of the Zunj, the black Basrawis, the remaining descendants of the great slave revolts, whose bands move through the streets beating cymbals, clapping their hands, and dancing the hayawa (Zunj dance).

I know that Basra will always stay alive in my memories. All these years, as long as I have talked about Basra, I have felt that it still alive at least in my mind. Now, as I connect the dots and put all this in writing about Basra (however much the light I cast it in appears to be one of fantasy, it is still a light gleaned from reality)-this Basra is from memory and distance, preserved in a time machine, will stay in my memory as long as I live and will pass it to my children and grandchildren because they will never experience what I had once upon a time.

If there is a disadvantage about to Basra it is the weather-- in summer the temperature soars to 100-110, sometimes even higher. The summer humidity is severe; thanks to all that scenic clear water. I could feel the warmth and the humidity of summer days besides the cooling system most homes used-Aaquol. This green cactus like plant from the desert was made to fit on the window from the outside. Water dripping on it would force a cool breeze and had a distinct smell that we loved.

Air-conditioning hardly makes things more than barely tolerable for many foreigners (even the Basrawis suffer), and that situation rules the city out as a place to visit from June to September. Another drawback-- though perhaps only temporary-- is that the suburbs of Basra to the west of the city are growing startlingly fast as the population explodes, and are therefore in urgent need of expert, careful town planning energetically applied: they are bloated, swelled up with an only partly digested influx of workers, technicians and administration men.

In our way to the Palm fields in a boat

Chapter 5

Chaldean Identity

"El'li ma andou atique ---ma andou jaded." He who does not hold on the ancient (old) will not be able to keep the new."
-An old Chaldean Proverb-

Schools of Dominicans Sisters called "Sisters of the Presentation"

We learned to be proud of our Chaldean culture through our families, church and school. I believe that history will judge us favorably. The simple question is "Are we willing to give up our identity, our culture, and our tradition?"

The simple answer should be.... No Wait, Not so fast.... Let's face it; we Iraqi people, in general, are religious people. Our primary goal is to create an environment through religious, social and educational means aimed at preserve, promote and process of continuing the culture, tradition and identity of the Chaldean Heritage. We bear responsibility to preserve a rich culture that is more than 6000 years old.

Chaldeans survived several conquerors and adapted to the new environment and prospered. The Greek, Persian, Turks and the Islamic Arab armies invaded Chaldea and conquered Iraq. No wonder we have different words that we use up to this time that refer to all these countries. We survived the Arab Islamic armies, who invaded Chaldea (the state of the Chaldeans) in 638 and proclaimed Islam as the official religion of the country and even changed the country's name to Iraq.

The Chaldeans had no choice but to adapt and they welcomed Arab rule that included mutual recognition between the two religions. The Chaldeans even adopted the Arabic language and no longer used Aramaic. The Chaldean population included bankers, physicians, engineers, astronomers, and translators.

We followed the footsteps of parents and grandparents who fought to survive as Chaldeans living in Iraq. We are proud to have such rich culture that is pure, filled with traditions. What we have is unique: the language culture and our identity-- and our delicious Iraqi food. Our mission is to pass on this culture to future generations.

What we remember from childhood we remember forever —
Permanent ghosts, stamped, inked, imprinted, eternally seen.
~ Cynthia Ozick ~

When I was six years old, my older sister and I were enrolled in the French school located in the old Basra with my older sister. There was a private bus that drove us back and forth to the first foreign languages I learned were French and Latin. I learned Latin in church attending Mass on a daily basis. In school I became fluent in French. My first language I learned was the French Language and Latin in church attending Mass was on a daily basis. In school my primary language was French with French nuns. Arabic was the second Language and this took place up to 8th grade. I was fluent in French and Mass was in Latin and I mastered.

The Dominican French nuns belonged to a congregation known as the "Sisters of the Presentation." I attended the same school that my grandmother attended. My dad would shower the nuns with dates during the season. Sister Antoinette was strict and toughest woman ever to wear a habit. You could tell by looking at her how mean she was. When we made a mistake during the piano lessons, our knuckles were brutally hit with the ruler for making a simple mistake or for not paying attention. My sister and I were treated well by the rest of the nuns because of my mom and my grandmother who attended the same school.

As Roman Catholics living in a Muslim country, we did not experience prejudice or disapproval. We attended Catholic schools run by French nuns, but we spoke Arabic at home. As young girls we were limited to our social life. We went twice a year to the movies with our uncle (my mother's brother) during the holidays. There was no television in Basra to watch the outside world.

The school had diverse students: Catholics, Jews and Muslims who came from wealthy families. The Jews struggled to get along with students in the public school, since the teaching of Islam was mandatory. Moreover, the Jewish students were not allowed to graduate from high school and were not given the high school diploma. I enjoyed the mixture and diversity of religions and learned from my friends about their different beliefs.

The school system was unique in many ways. As a student I had no choice of what courses to take. The first grade mandatory courses were math, grammar, history, geography, biology, gym, life-skills, and crafts. In the fourth grade geometry, algebra, and chemistry were included.

School requirements were much more difficult than those in other countries. I tried both the British system and the American System. The French system in Basra was the hardest. Schooling was hard work and little fun. Yet we were happy growing up. Our parents made sure that we got what we needed including love and affection.

One of the interesting aspects of growing up in an environment where the world participates in your everyday life almost as much as you do is to distinguish reality from legend. The nuns knew the whole family, the lay teachers such as Mademoiselle Marow knew the family and students' parents knew the family. This made it necessary for me to do well in my homework and be on my best respectful behavior.

During lunch time when we were sitting on benches chatting during the break and one of nuns passed us, it was a required courtesy for good behavior to stand up out of respect and greet the nuns or the teachers and say "Bonjour, ma soeur. . . or Bonjour, mademoiselle...." Respect was a must. These things came naturally without hard work or questions by us or other students. Now, looking back, I appreciate being in this elite elementary school.

The school uniform was distinct. Ours was the only school in Basra that required uniforms. The school buses were private and as students we never mingled with the students from public schools.

At this elite school with students were a mixture of three ethnic groups: Catholics like us who came from an upper middle class, Jewish students who were privileged and favored the Catholic Schools for their reputation. The third group was the rich Muslims who believed in the goodness of Christian teaching and upbringing. Very few came to the school for having been expelled or disqualified for further education in the public schools.

Lunch in the Middle East (Iraq) was the main and the heaviest meal of the day. The schools had three lunch options. The first: students ate hot meals in the school cooked and served by the nuns. The second option was for those who wished to go home to eat. They were taken back and forth by bus. The third option was the students to bring one's own lunch.

Most of the students brought sandwiches for lunch. Very few ate a hot meal at school because no one liked what was served. I remember that my sister and I were different in this matter from the other students. There were several profound memories being in this school that made my sister and I different than other students. My parents never believed in sandwiches for lunch. My mother cooked fresh food daily and she sent us hot meals every day with our servant (Khalaf) who drove his bike to get us the hot food in time for lunch. Some, who lived close by within walking distance went home for lunch.

I had a deal with my older sister when the lunch was delivered to us. I like fruits over lunch, so the plan was that I would eat the fruit and my sister would eat the lunch. After we were done, one of us would take the empty lunch box to the servant who waited to take the lunch box (sufertas) back to my home. The lunch box style was famous in the far eastern cultures; it was made out of stainless steel round compartments with four layers one on top of the other. Each compartment had different foods, such as rice, meat, gravy, vegetables, and desert with fruits on the side.

I believe that I had a good start and since other girls were also from affluent families able to fit right in." The French nuns were Dominicans sisters called. These missionaries started Catholic Schools in the Muslim worlds to strengthen the Christian faith. The Sisters of the Dominican order had its presence in Iraq since the 1800s.

On the other hand, my husband who was born and raised in Baghdad attended The American Jesuits School who had been in Baghdad for 37 years. They were famous for Baghdad College and Al-Hikma University and were accepted by the Iraqi government as well by Iraqi families. The Baghdad Jesuit effort made them be accused by the Iraqi government on the interaction between young American Jesuits and youthful Iraqi citizens and their families against the government.

The American Jesuits were very popular in Iraq and Lebanon. Boarding students—Christian, Jewish, and Muslim came to their schools from all over Iraq where there was boarding program for students coming from other Iraqi cities they accommodated all Christian, Jewish and Muslim students.

Play Louis the XVI at school in Basra. My best friend and I
The Dominican French nuns belonged to a congregation
known "Sisters of the Presentation"

My best Chaldean friend Najla and myself

Chapter 6

Old Stories with Afternoon Tea

"I had the good fortune to live in Iraq for a couple of years in the mid sixties just before Saddam Hussein seized power. It was one of the most civilized and peaceful, well-run countries I have ever visited. Baghdad in those days was cleaner and safer than most European cities. The people at every level were friendly and hospitable. Everything that has happened since the war was totally predictable even to an untrained bystander like myself."
Trevor Bailey, I.O.W. UK

Growing in Iraq during the fifties and sixties was something I do not believe that others who read this book will ever could imagine. Iraq was called "Cross Roads" between Europe and India and China. From earliest times it was a strategic and economic center. You would think it was a fairytale.

*"There are few hours in life
more agreeable than the hour
dedicated to the ceremony
known as afternoon tea."*
-Henry James-

China is considered the birthplace of tea. However, years ago, people who dwell in desert climates drank plenty of hot tea to cool off. The reasoning, as I understood it, was that drinking hot liquids would force you to sweat more, thus making the body cooler and bringing it to a comfortable temperature. Although the custom of drinking tea dates back to the third millennium BC in China, Arabs also used tea during the same time in the desert. Black tea was served in a clear glass cups without milk and just a bit of sugar.

It was not until the mid- seventeenth century that tea first appeared in England. Anna, Duchess of Bedford, introduced afternoon tea in the year 1840. The Duchess would become hungry around four o'clock in the afternoon. The evening meal in her household was served fashionably late at eight o'clock, thus leaving a long period of time between lunch and dinner.

The Duchess asked that a tray of tea, bread and butter (sometime earlier, the sandwich makers had the idea of putting a filling between two slices of bread) and cake be brought to her room during the late afternoon. This became a habit of hers and she began inviting friends to join her. This pause for tea became a fashionable social event. During the 1880's, upper-class and society women would change into long gowns, gloves and hats for their afternoon tea, which was usually served in the drawing room between four and five o'clock.

Afternoon Tea Tradition

Traditional Iraqi afternoon tea consisted of a selection of dainty sandwiches (including thinly sliced cheese sandwiches), scones served with clotted cream and preserves. Cakes and pastries were also served. Besides the famous baked khubuz, the best snacks during the mid day with afternoon tea (Chi) were freshly baked Ka'ak and Baksam (similar to biscotti) brought fresh from the bakery. They were addictive.

The British brought to Basra the English Tradition of the afternoon teatime. However the Iraqi culture used tea grown in Ceylon (Sri-Lanka) poured from silver tea pot into delicate bone china cups. This is a British tradition was adopted by the Basrawies who became well known in other parts of Iraq for being tea drinkers.

Traditionally, **in Iraq** tea, was a daily routine in the morning and afternoon. It was also served in offices where a special employee was hired just to serve tea to the other employees and their business guests. This tea server's job was to make tea and serve it and wash the cups. In Arabic he was called chi-chi.

My memories take me back to my childhood when my mother and her sisters, and sometimes their female friends got together around 4 or 5 p.m. for afternoon tea. Loose tea with hot milk (not cream) was served with small tea finger sandwiches, small cakes, pastries and thick cream, butter and assorted jams of the season. Teas were for showing off more than anything else. The host served the guests from a small cart while sitting and enjoying food and conversation. This type of tea is known as the Low tea, since it was served in the low part of the afternoon and only small bites were served, rather than a large spread.

I remember when I was a child my grandmother used to pour the tea in the saucer to cool before I was able to drink it to make sure I did not get burned. It was the most enjoyable drink to me at that time. This is the one that comes to mind when people think of English tea ceremonies. It all began back as tradition, but later became a ritual and tea became the 'in-thing' for the upper-class women.

Tea is usually the black tea served with milk (never cream) and sometimes with sugar. Strong tea served with lots of milk and often two teaspoons of sugar, usually in a cup and a saucer.

Tea Ritual

Even very slightly formal events can be a cause for cups and saucers to be used instead of mugs. A typical semi-formal tea ritual might run as follows:

1. Use a kettle to boil and water, poured into a teapot.
2. Water is swirled around the pot to warm it and then poured out.
3. Loose tealeaves is added to the pot while the kettle is re-boiled, cardamom seeds are added.
4. The pot is allowed to brew for several minutes. The stove is turned off to let the tea settle for five minutes.
5. A tea strainer, like a miniature sieve, is placed over the top of a clean teapot and the tea is poured into the teapot.
6. Tea is poured into individual cups and saucers ready to serve the guests.

7. The straight black tea is then offered to guests who choose to add warm milk and sugar to their taste.
8. The pot will normally hold enough tea so as not to be empty after filling the cups of all the guests. Usually re-fills are offered and the teapot is put aside covered with a tea cozy which is replaced after everyone has been served.

Whether to put milk into the cup before or after the tea has been a matter of some debate. My middle son Mahir usually would put the milk and sugar, stir and then add the tea. Certain delicate cups sometimes need to put the spoon in the cup before pouring the tea. The sudden heat of the tea decreases the heat that prevents cracking the cups.

This tradition has been handed down from generations. However, some hold that adding milk second tends to scald the milk. This affects the taste and so, for best taste, the warm milk should be poured first.

There is also a proper etiquette in drinking tea when using a cup and saucer. The cup and saucer should be lifted together from the table with the left hand on the saucer and the right on the handle of the cup. The right hand should then lift the cup away from the saucer to be drunk before replacing it. This rule is relaxed when having tea at a dining table, as opposed to having tea in armchairs, etc. Drinking tea from the saucer (poured from the cup in order to cool it) was not uncommon at one time, but is now almost universally considered a breach of etiquette.

Adults and children love to drink tea. When we were young, we loved to drink the tea and my mother or my grandmother would pour some in the saucer and allow me to sip the tea. Now since I have my own grandchildren they always ask "Nana can you make us some Chi-Chi is the name for tea in Arabic as well in Hindi (India) and they know always the answer is "yes." I do not mind since I serve them decaffeinated tea made with teabags since they do not like the loose tea and I have not yet seen decaffeinated loose tea.

When you have a large group you might serve tea in a (Samwer) in Arabic often of brass, with a spigot near its base, widely used in Russia to boil water for tea. In traditional samovars water is heated by means of a vertical tube, containing burning charcoal, running up the middle of the urn. A filled teapot is set atop the chimney to steep. A lighter brew can be obtained by adding more water to the teacup from the spigot. Traditionally, a samovar was used for all household needs that required hot water, and almost all families possessed one in silver or stainless steal or copper. This large container sits on four short legs.

It is said that the samovar culture is well suited to tea drinking in a communal setting over a protracted period. The Russian expression "to have a sit by samovar" means to have a leisurely talk while drinking tea from a samovar. Like the Middle Eastern, using the argil culture or with the Japanese tea ceremony" Japanese tea ceremony.

Azerbaijan unearthed a ceramic samovar-like utensil identified by a characteristic central tube covered with soot, suggesting it was heated from the inside. It didn't look like modern samovars, though. In particular, the tube was open from the bottom, suggesting that it was placed over a fire like an ordinary pot. There were similar devices found in Iran and China.

Personally I prefer cool rather than hot tea. After boiling the water, I need to wait at least fifteen minutes for it to cool down enough so that I won't burn myself. My family members start drinking it after about five minutes. My tongue gets this burned feeling that stays for 2-3 days if I drink it that hot. One can get accustomed to hot tea, however, just as one can get used to spicy foods

These cups used for plain tea only

Cups and saucers are used when serving milk with tea

This is a classic customary tea time setting

(Samwer) in Arabic or (Samovar) in Turkish and Russian.

Chapter 7

A trip to Lebanon

In June in the early fifties during the summer vacation, my parents made arrangements for a trip to Lebanon, renting a large house in the mountains for us to stay for three months. We were four children in our family and other two close to our ages my mother's, sister children. We were going to meet other several families from Basra—friends of my parents who also rented homes in the area.

We started the trip from Basra by taking the train to Baghdad from the Central Railway Station which is by itself was a great journey. We had private sleeping compartments and it was air-conditioned. This train was built during the World War I by the British to connect Iraq cities with Syria and Turkey. The Journey from Basra-Baghdad took 12 hours in the diesel-powered engine. We left Basra around 6 pm and the train passed overnight through cities across Iraq and made several stops on the way to drop and pick-up passengers. Security was great and we heard my parents talking to the security control personal and he assured my parents that it was always safe.

My mother had brought sandwiches, fruits, snacks and drinks. After we ate we changed into our nightgowns and slept. The sound of the train sound made us sleep well. In the early morning before the sunrise, we were awakened by noises of the peasant women who raise water buffalo and sell fresh yogurt and Gaimar to the train passengers as the train passes their area in the morning. That was the best breakfast on the train, and we always looked forward to it. After we finished eating our breakfast, we drank hot tea brought to us by the train security was in-charge of our cabin.

Then we started changing and watching the train passing the cities along the way and stopping in some areas for people to get off. By 9 in the morning, my parents said that we were soon going to reach the Baghdad station. When we arrived, my uncle Yousif (My father's brother) and his two boys (Faiz and Basil) were there to meet us.

Baghdad seemed a big city that someone could get lost in. There was a lot of traffic: cars, horse-drawn carriages and buses moves up and down the streets used for transportations. Baghdad is the capital of Iraq, as tall buildings and houses with large gardens. The weather was warm and dry not like Basra, which is hot and humid. As we reached my uncle's house his wife greeted us by the door welcoming us to the house, wanting to make us feel comfortable. She made sure that our two younger cousins were younger than us were behaving. We were three older girls and my brother who was the youngest-- 2 years old.

My uncle's house was crowded that day with friends and relatives visiting our family. For us children it was fun, especially when we played marbles. Young boys played marbles. but we girls learned the game by watching boys playing. Soon it was time to bathe and go to sleep since we had a full schedule for the next day to visit several places in the city of Baghdad.

Just as at home, we slept on the flat roof. The weather in Baghdad was pleasant and cooler at night than the weather in Basra. I enjoyed the night sleep, counting the stars surrounding the half moon in the sky as I kept moving my legs to the cool spots on my bed. While we kids were talking, we started falling asleep one after the other.

As the sun was rising, I started moving in my bed, getting away from the heat of the sun to enjoy the cool breeze of early morning, just as the cuckoo began a familiar, song. The brown and white bird with its black flap was standing by a high wall. A the sound of the bird's song, we all started singing with the bird:

"Cuckoo ikhti, cuckoo ikhti, wayne ikhti?
[cuckoo, cuckoo, where is my sister?]

The bird chirrups:
"Bil Hilla"
[At Hilla]

We kept repeating the song with the birds until they disappeared when the sun got hot. We ran down the stairs as we were called for breakfast. After washing and dressing up, we were on our way for breakfast in the garden.

What a cute little place! I have heard from my parents about the gardens in Baghdad, I knew this would be a nice experience. This was the first time I visited my uncle's house. Immediately I noticed the flowers and garden gazzibo, the fresh flowers sitting at the table, and the elegant china for our tea. The presentation was breath taking tea with milk, Gaimer (Clotted cream/Devonshire Cream) several home made jams, cheeses, fresh baked bread, tomato and goat cheese, cucumber, fresh mint/basil, some pastries and fresh fruits.

We were seated under a large grape vine canapé/Gazebo that provided shade, as well as protection from the birds. The early morning was so peaceful and serene with the noise of the birds and the sound of water from the fountain. All the fruit trees and their blossoms and the flowers under those trees brought an aroma smells like a bouquet of flowers.

The surroundings enhanced our enjoyment of breakfast, after which the adults helped to clear everything to inside the house since we needed to get ready to visit some landmarks in Baghdad.

We visited the Al Rashid Street is located in downtown Baghdad. It is considered one of the oldest streets in Baghdad. Al Rasheed Street or Al Rashid Street is located in downtown Baghdad and is one of the city's main streets, stretching from North Gate to South Gate. The origin of Al Rasheed Street goes back to the Ottomans who ruled Iraq from 1534 to 1918. During that time, the only known public street in Baghdad was Al Naher Street (Sharih al-Naher). Al Naher means River - the street stretching a few kilometers along the east banks of the river.

Al Naher Street, was known for up-scale merchandize from cosmetics to fashion stores for women and children, as well as and accessories for men. It also had a large section exclusively for imported designer fabrics for fashionable women's clothing. A few very small stores offered imported fashion outfits.

In 1917, Al Rasheed Street was the first street to be decorated with lights in Baghdad city. However, my mother informed my aunt that she kept her shopping excursions for Beirut since prices there were reasonable, and Lebanon was famous with for Parisian fashions that came directly after Paris.

After spending some time window-shopping, my uncle decided to take us for late lunch to a beautiful restaurant located on the Tigris River. It was not a surprise to us since it was like the Shat-Al-Arab in Basra. The Tigris, however, had buildings on both sides and Shat-Al-Arab had the coffee houses on one side and the palm fields across the other side of Shat-Al-Arab (River)

When we were at the middle of the boulevard (Abu Nawas) we were able to see the bright reflection of the sun in the clear river across the water. This mile long boulevard, which runs along the east bank of the Tigris, is famous for the magnificent fish (masguf) served. Music from numerous coffee houses adds to the surrounding joy and festivity. There were tables and chairs along the riverbank filled with people relaxing and enjoying the charm, beauty and the coolness of day.

Uncle Yousif talked to the boatman in one of the coffee houses and ordered a large live (Shabout) fish to be cleaned washed and sprinkled with salt and spices and then cooked on fire lit with twigs and branches from fruit trees. When the blaze of flames dies down, that means the fire is ready to cook the fish. The boatman, then would lay the fish on the hot glowing ashes and embers. We spent some time watching the fishing and the cooking process.

My mother suggested that we return to the house since she was worried that we might be tired. Then we headed to the house since we would be leaving for Beirut, Lebanon, the following day. After dinner that day we were asked to go to sleep early since we had to wake up early the next day to pack and prepare to leave.

The next morning we woke up early, had breakfast and packed our luggage, ready to leave in the afternoon. My father and his brother Yousif left after breakfast to take care of business, such as banking and last minute shopping for the road.

Time went so fast and we were ready on schedule to go to the bus station to pick up the bus to Beirut via Damascus/Syria. We learned that the trip would take about 15 hours. We arrived to the bus station ...WOW... It was an extremely large/gigantic bus called Nairn.

NARIN COACHE (Called the desert bus): The first class trailer had luxurious accommodates 20 passengers for overnight journey. We traveled on to Lebanon in the early fifties. It would have been hard to describe it since I was only (7) years old at that time. My recollection of the Nairn had similar adjustable seats and the inside was like an airplane. That was a fabulous bus and that the trip was very comfortable air-conditioned despite a 15-17 hour ride.

Damascus is the capital of Syria and is the oldest city in the world. Barada River flows through the city of Damascus. I remember that the hotel was over looking the Barada River. While visiting Damascus for four days, we visited the souq (bazaar) that my parents were interested in. We also took a city tour, to churches (St. Annias) and mosques (Umayyad).

Our stay in Damascus was short. As children we had more fun in the hotel since it was cool there while watching the boats on the river Barada from the hotel balcony.

Day four in Damascus: we packed at night to leave for Lebanon where we would be spending the rest of the summer vacation. My parents hired a taxi van to take us to Lebanon. The travel time was two hours. We stopped to take pictures at the borders.

Three Months in Lebanon

Lebanon was occupied by the French: under a League of Nations mandate after the Ottoman Empire was defeated in World War I (1914-1918) and the port of Lebanon became the gateway to the world During World War II (1939-1945).

Lebanon became an independent republic and for three decades prospered under a free-market economy. However, the country experienced increasing hostility among rival religious groups, especially between Christians and Muslims. Lebanon was the only Christian country in the Middle East where Christians from all the surrounding countries visited Lebanon during the summer seasons. Beirut is Lebanon's capital, principal port, and largest city.

The experience of coming out of Syria, a stunning yet underdeveloped country, across miles of flat desert into a sea of mountainous green, with cooler air, and a more relaxed atmosphere, was breathtaking. The contrasts between the two countries did not end there - Lebanon is full of banks, one on every corner it seems that in Lebanon there it was impossible to get money out of a bank. Commercialization and modern living in the form of neon signs and the Golden Arches were everywhere.

The Capital is Beirut and the home to six universities: the well-known American University of Beirut; the Jesuit-sponsored Saint Joseph University; the government-supported Lebanese University; the Egyptian-sponsored Beirut Arab University; the Lebanese American University; and the Armenian Hagazian College. Lebanon also has more than 100 technical, vocational, and other Specialized Schools for specialty students.

A Cultural Contrast at Every Turn

Lebanon is the only country where you can swim in the Mediterranean Sea and ski on the mountains on the same day. The Cedars of Lebanon, famous since Biblical times, are now protected in a few mountain groves. Arabic is the official language of the country, and is even spoken by the minority population of Lebanese. The Armenian population speaks mostly Armenian or Turkish, while Assyrians speak Syriac. French and English are also widely spoken. A land of varied terrain, Lebanon encompasses coastline, mountain, and fertile growing regions such as the Bekáa Valley, which is a primary cereal-producing region. The population of the country is made up of ethnic groups from every Middle Eastern country, a political situation that reflects Lebanon's long history.

Beirut was often referred to as the "Paris of the Middle East;" others called the country "Switzerland of the Middle East." Beirut was also considered the commercial center of the Middle East. Lebanon is named for the major mountain range that runs north to south through the middle of the country. Christians, who were the majority, always ruled Lebanon's government. Lately Muslims and Christians have many sectarian subdivisions. The Druze, Christians, include the Marinates, the Eastern Orthodox, Mel kites (Greek Catholics) Armenians, and Protestants.

Various government offices are still reserved for specific sects: the prime minister is always a Sunni Muslim; the president is always a Marinate, (Christian) and the speaker of the house is always a Shiite.

I was not sure what to expect when we approached Beirut, but the view was spectacular. Descending the Chough Mountains via some winding roads, the tall buildings of rebuilt Beirut glistened far below. Behind them, a setting sun immersed the Mediterranean into a sea of orange. Car horns blared - welcome to the Mercedes capital of the Middle East.

Beirut, the Lebanese capital behind lies the "Bekaa Valley" and in the North the Syrian Desert is stretched out. Our taxi continued heading to the mountain where the house we are going to live in through the summer.

It was around early evening as we arrived to the house. The scenery and the trees surrounding the home were dramatic and breathtaking with impressive sundown dramatic views. The elderly woman, who was the owner of the house, came out of to greet us, to make us comfortable and show my parents the house and to see whether they needed anything. She also described to my parents the way to the souk where we could do the grocery shopping. Lebanese made their living by renting their homes for the season and the rent money would support them financially for the next winter. She had a small room to sleep in by the garage and she had an outdoor wood grill where she cooked her food.

We helped to take our luggage down from the car and followed our parents to guide us to our bedrooms. We were instructed to shower before it got late, to have a good night sleep in order to wake up early in the morning. We were extremely tired and we were asleep right away. In Lebanon we could sleep indoors with light blankets to cover ourselves. It was a good night sleep.

The next morning I was the first one to wake up. I was curious to see the outside in the morning with the crack of dawn. The old woman was already outside making tea and grilling onions. The aroma was significant; every time I smell grilled onion my memories take me back to Lebanon. Everyone started waking up and we started dressing up to go out as our driver was there to pick us up to go to the market and then we would go to Beirut.

As we passed the souk, my parents decided to do the shopping on the way back.

Our driver was explaining to my parents about all the small villages we were passing and how each village is unique and famous for its individuality, each different from the others. Along the road there were stands with the seasonal fruits for sale and my dad would ask the driver to stop for fresh fruits and vegetables that had been cut on the same day. There were usually water faucets along the road to wash the fruits and vegetables. By the time we arrived home, most of the fruits and vegetables were gone.

The Beirut Corniche

My father arranged with a van driver to pick us up from the house to downtown Beirut on the days that my mother and aunts want to go shopping. Beirut was famous for upscale shopping because the fashionable goods came from Paris in the same year. My dad would take the children to the Corniche to swim in the Mediterranean Sea.

Our day started in a street café in Beirut. Over Arabian coffee and croissants, we enjoyed the summer day that was pleasant and not hot. We wandered down the Corniche, an impressive coastal strip, where people like to stroll and pose at sunset. Speedboats were nearer the shore; all along the Corniche people were jogging, doing fitness routines, fishing or diving into the sea; children were playing badminton, or cyclists were travelling at impossible speeds while still avoiding pedestrians, street sellers and shoeshine boys were trying to make a living; young lovers walked hand in hand, and the endless roar and honking of traffic could be heard. It was calming and relaxing.

After arriving in Beirut, we still had some time; so we plunged into the cultural life of the lively capital. Beirut is once more beginning to bloom. You can feel and see the excitement everywhere. When we first ramble through the city, the influences of the different cultures become apparent. We are greeted with effusive cordiality: "Where are you from?" we are often asked. The reactions to our answers are exceedingly friendly: "Oh Iraq, welcome to Lebanon. "Have a nice time." At first we were surprised at the friendliness, since we were told that Lebanon was about spending money. But we found that nobody wanted to sell us anything or con us. The people were simply unbelievably friendly and obliging!

On the way to the beach we discovered that the district of 'Centre-Ville' (Down Town), was beautiful and busy with people. The mixture of Arabian and Italian Baroque architecture was built lovingly over a long period of construction. The first street cafés and shops brought life into the city centre. In the cafés you could believe yourself to be right in Paris, especially at the sight of the attractive Lebanese ladies.

My mother, her sisters and friends came back from shopping with many large shopping bags, saying that they were hungry. My dad suggested we go to a nice restaurant that was famous for rotisserie chicken and Meza. This was a traditional Lebanese restaurant. In the restaurants there are up to forty different appetizers (Meza) which are consumed with flat bread. Olive oil pickles, sesame pastes, grilled vegetables, different sorts of salad—all so lavish that everyone is full by the time the main course is served.

This was a typical day in Lebanon other than visiting different villages such as Baalbeck, an ancient city with its magnificent landscape; Beit-ed-dine is one of the most precious and treasured Arabic agricultural historical palace with a magnificent fountain in the centre; Zahle was founded in the 18th century.

The buildings with red tiled roof were created on the shores of "al Bardawni" river. Nowadays, restaurants, coffee-rooms and old houses flourish on each river. Harissa specifically for the view and it did not disappoint. We climbed the monument to get the best view of Beirut and the sea below. This is a large statue of the Holly Mary facing the sea.

This trip was the first time for me. Later, I visited Lebanon several times from Baghdad and quite few times from the States, and I can never have enough of it.

"Zahle" *by the water fall , my mom, aunts, Uncle,*
cousins, sisters, me and my family friends

Harisa-Lebanon Statue of Mary
facing the Mediterranean Sea.

My father in Lebanon
–Zahle Restaurant

Cooling down by the waterfall stream in a restaurant

Chapter 8

To acquire knowledge, one must study; but to acquire
wisdom, one must observe.
-Marilyn vos Savant-

My Relationship With My Grandmother

Children in Iraq expected to listen to their elders. As my grandparents once said to me," We all for good realize that our life has a meaning, and we will leave a legacy. Especially when grandchildren look up to their elders.

My grandmother from my mother's side was gentle and kind. She was always in a good mood. When she spoke, her words came in a very soft tone of voice. I was told that she lived in an orphanage with her mother and younger sister. In those days if the husband (father) died, the wife had no means of financial support, especially when she had no other family. That's why my great grandmother chose to stay at the orphanage and work to stay with her two daughters. My grandmother spoke Arabic, Chaldean and French.

After several years my grandfather wanted to get married. He approached the nuns to ask if they knew a girl that he might be able to marry. At that time there was no dating and since he had no family to direct him to the right girl, he reached out to the nuns since they were raising orphans. Since my grandfather was well known in Basra working at the Othman Bank and used to help the nuns raise money for their orphanage, he approached one of the nuns to say that he was interested in getting married and was there a young girl that would be a good match for him. The nun promised my grandfather that she would keep an eye out for such a girl.

A few weeks passed and the nun made a visit to the bank where my grandfather worked. She was happy to recommend a girl whose mother also worked and lived at the orphanage. My grandfather was interested in marriage and went to the convent and asked the Mother Superior for permission to marry the girl. Mother Superior said to my grandfather that this girl would fit with him since she was educated and could speak French. My grandfather was happy with the match and they were married and her mother and sister moved in with them.

I found out that listening to my grandmother made me more mature than my other siblings. I learned from my elders and became alert all the time knowing of my surroundings. I listened to their experiences as they shared their wisdom in many ways. It makes sense of who I am. I learned a lot from my grandmother, mother and aunts who were very wise and intelligent women.

I remember that I liked a particular story that I kept asking her to tell me over and over about her stepfather who was blind due to his diabetes and yet he did everything like a normal man. He had a special talent for working with musical instruments, especially working as a piano tuner, and used to give private lessons teaching piano to wealthy families.

She told me that after her mother died, her stepfather decided to take his younger stepdaughter to a boarding school in India. My grandmother who was pregnant with my mother, and her stepbrother who was three years, old accompanied my great grandfather.

My grandmother said that I enjoyed the story more when I realized that her stepfather was creative, independent, and never needed help from others. According to my grandmother, he tied his three- year old with a rope at his waist to make sure that he did not lose him on the ship.

My grandmother continued with the story about the trip when they took a passenger boat to New Delhi in India to enroll my great aunt in a boarding school. After they made sure that my great aunt was in good hands with the nuns in school, they were on their way back to Basra, Iraq, when my grandmother realized that she was going to have to give birth to a baby girl. My mother's birth in India made them extend their stay in New Delhi.

My grandmother used to tell me, "If you don't know where you come from, how will you know where you are going? How will you know where you belong?" Some days my memory is clear; on other days it's cloudy. On the good days, I ask her about the people in the photographs and we discuss the old documents. While she talks, I never thought to take notes, but everything stayed in my mind. Slowly I say a silent prayer. Thank you, Lord, for allowing me this time to connect with my grandmother and in the process to discover some of my family history.

Unconditional Love

> *"Gone yet not forgotten, Although we are apart,*
> *Your spirit lives within me forever in my heart."*

This poem was written because of a beautiful lady that gave unconditional love to her children and grandchildren, a legacy of her faith that was passed from her mother. I had the honor and privilege to have the wisdom, knowledge and the love for God passed down from these two women. God blessed me with the love of a grandmother as well as a mother to shape my life.

They truly were the lighthouses God sent me to ensure that I would one day grow to love him as much as they did, and to share with the grandchildren that would one day grace my own life. Their lights continue to guide and show me the unconditional love that flows from God through them I would hear her in the kitchen and go downstairs in the early morning. She would make herself and everyone else tea. She would wrap one of her sweaters around me and we would go sit outside.

Mama Jose (Grandmother) sits in the balcony to enjoy her tea and I would show her how fast I could run around the house in my pajamas and tell her all about Story Hour at the library. Mama Jose was always great because she would listen to me go on about my six-year-old world and treat me as if I were older, even though I was really just a kid who wore slippers and could never eat too many cheese sandwiches with a hot cup of tea. I guess you could say that my grandmother is one of my heroes. I remember seeing her when she served my grandfather with his meal.

She would stand by the table looking for his approval and waiting in case he needed a drink of water or waiting for any suggestion he might have. She respected him. She never sat and ate with him. She always ate with the children and grandchildren. It was only on special days and Sundays the family ate together.

It seems like an exaggeration, but I believe it's true. I define a hero as a person who taught me about life and how to treat self and others. As I was growing up, Mama Jose was still there and she still listens and treats me as important, as if I were more than the person that I am and have become. She sits outside with me, and now I am almost as tall as she is, and she tells me about her life and listens to mine.

She told me about my mom when she was young and about when she was little and how she learned sewing on her own at age 13. Mama Jose would always play my little kid games with me and she never ignored me. That means a lot to me and it always has.

When I was little, I don't think I saw that, but now as I am writing, my memories are coming back to and I can see vividly. My grandmother treated me like a person and that has meant a great deal to me. When I sat outside with her, she used to ask about my school and friends I knew she really cared. She was my grandmother after all. And just for that, just for that simple fact, I loved her more than words or actions can describe.

Tribute to my Grandmother

My mother always kept me away as I earlier since my older sister was jealous of me and my mother always tried to separate us. When I was eight years old I stayed with my grandmother. My older sister used to fight with me all the time. My grandmother asked my mom to allow me to stay with her. She loved me so much. Every morning my grandmother would wake up and make me breakfast and my mother would send my lunch to school.

On a spring day morning, I woke up as usual and my grandmother had my breakfast ready as usual. I left my grandparent's house and my grand mother Mama Jose said goodbye to me and she kissed me on my forehead.

I was walking toward the neighbor's home where other two girlfriends were also waiting for the school bus. Suddenly a car made a fast turn at the road. It was my younger uncle speeding and my friends asked me what was wrong with him. I said that he was my uncle. Soon after, we saw the bus coming and we forgot about my uncle since we were going on picnic trip on a boat across the river to the palm fields.

It was a great picnic. I enjoyed the boat ride with my friends as well as the field where we played different games including hide and seek. The teachers and the nuns made sure that all the girls were having a good time and being safe. After lunch we went for a walk exploring the fields and looking at different fruit trees. Toward the end of the day, our chaperones gathered us and we said the prayer to get home safe. We took the boat back to the marina.

As the boat was docking I noticed my father waiting for me. I ran to him asking why he was there. I was supposed to return home by bus. His answer was that, "You are coming home with me because Mama Josa is sick." My mother was at the house to receive us when we were dropped at the house. I started crying, saying that she was well when I left this morning. My dad tried to explain that she became sick after I left to take the bus.

My dad then talked to the teacher for me to take the bus and stay with my best friend Najla and then my parents would pick me up later that evening. I have no memories about staying at my friends that day (my friend told me that I spent the time at her house). I was preoccupied with my grandmother being sick. How could my Mama Jose be sick and die. When I left her house, she was OK.

After few hours my dad came to my friend's house and picked me up to go home. Since my grandmother's house was closer to my friend's house my dad said that we would stop and pick up my mom and go home. I was puzzled and did not figure out what was going on.

However, upon our arrival and as I entered the house, there were lots of people and my mom started screaming with a cry, "Salma, no more Mama Jose." I started going through the rooms looking for her when my grandfather came to me and took me aside telling me that she had a stroke and the doctor was not able to help her get well. I said to him that I wanted to see her. His reply was she was already buried. Immediately I ran toward my mother asking her why they did not wait for me to see her before the burial. Everyone was crying and the shock was overwhelming for everyone-- young and old. She was a good woman and she touched everyone in town since she was well known and as good and young.

My grandmother's death affected me emotionally and I cannot forget the day of the incident. Every time I think about the event, I choke with tears. I was unable to believe that what happened was real. I was not accepting it.

Later on, I understood that the tradition was to bury the dead before sundown. The whole town of Basra was in shock since she was young (46 years old). My grandmother's death was all over town and people were visiting her home, many were former and current church members of congregations where the family attended the Mass and where my grandfather was the head of the ushers.

By the next few days the family was receiving telegrams from all over. Some friends of mine had a common theme. In addition to expressing their sympathy they all said that they felt they had known my grandmother: "We remember your grandmother from the stories you would tell us about her."

These are the kinds of memories we all cling to. They can be collective, shared, or private. They may be special moments -- remembrances of her as a sister, a wife, a mother, or a friend. But when we share those memories, they become a part of someone else. The memories become the possession of others. Today, I want to share just a few memories of my grandmother.

Her determination showed in the way she cared for people. I can't remember a time when I spoke to her, when she didn't remind me that she said a prayer for all of her children and grandchildren. She was determined to make prayer a part of her life. I must confess that some smells often evoke memories for me. That is especially true for the smells of foods.

The most vivid memory of my grandmother is the picture of her during Christmas when she cooked the lamb with yellow rice with saffron. When I smell this type of food I remember the many meals that she cooked and the times I spent at her house during the holidays. Fried chicken and stuffed grape leaves bring back memories of Sunday dinner at her house after church.

Growing up next door to her meant a lot to my immediate family since we spent a great deal of time at her house. Indeed, we lived at her house until my father finished building ours. Sometimes children stay and are in need of discipline.

My grandmother being pregnant with my mother.

Chapter 9

LIVING in Basra The whole time during my childhood my parents and grandparents would talk about how in the old days — meaning the days before Saddam's Baath Party took over — there were mourning processions to mark Ashora, which is the memory of the death of Imam Hussein Bin Ali, the grandson of the Prophet Muhammad. This was the battle of Karbala, where Hussein was killed, and stories describing his assassination.

People would spend what they could for these meals. The poor might only serve water or juices, while wealthy people hired specialty chefs for the occasion to perfect the meals. And some cooks offered their services for free, seeking forgiveness or reward, instead.

Throughout the 40-day mourning period, people served a variety of foods. As a child, I used to take an empty pot and leave it by the front door so that when the Shea neighbors bring us the harisa, I ask them to pour it into my pot. I always looked forward to the day of Ashora despite its tragic associations. Everybody in my neighborhood shared the food regardless of his or her religious belief and background.

People would spend what they could for these meals. The poor might only serve water or juices, while wealthy people hired specialty chefs for the occasion to perfect the meals. And some cooks offered their services for free, seeking God's forgiveness or getting a reward, instead.

Salma Ajo, Ph.D

Why Ashura is significant for Shea:

Ashura is significant for Shea because it is a time of morning for the Husain bin Ali, the grandson of Muhammad who he was killed with members of his family and close friends at the Battle of Karbala in the year (680 AD).

I remember vividly the prayers from the loud speaker at night until midnight. Men and women wore black for ten days and attended the prayers on the streets. The commemoration was always a sad period of time for Shiites where the streets were blocked and covered with carpets for the event. For Shea is a sad timing.

During this time Shea refrain from music, since the Arabic culture generally considers music impolite during death rituals. It is a time for sorrow and respect for the person's passing away, and it is also a time for self-reflection, when one commits oneself to the mourning of the Husain. During this time people never make plans for weddings and parties on this date.

Throughout the evening they express mourning by crying and listening to poems about the tragedy and sermons on how Husain and his family were martyred. This is intended to connect them with Husain's suffering, and the sacrifices he made to keep Islam alive.

But among all these festivities, I still wondered about the missing part: the prohibited mourning processions and plays of the battle in which Imam Hussein was slaughtered.

The mourning processions and marchers were very moving and exotic to my eyes, but more important was the wave of drastic change that just started sweeping the streets.

Rich and poor families set money every year to provide food to pilgrims and sometimes the entire neighborhoods stayed up all night on the day of Ashore, preparing the harissa and my family has never cooked for that occasion. The day of Ashore and the entire 40-day mourning period were among the best memories of my childhood. I enjoyed watching people cooking everywhere. They stayed up all night preparing their *harissa,* a giant porridge made of lamb and ground soaked wheat. The harissa was distributed to all the neighbors --Muslims and others.

Living side by side with Muslims, we respected their holidays and celebrations and they did the same with us where they would be sharing their feeling with the Christians and Jews. As a matter of fact we looked forward to these events.

Shiite men in Baghdad and Basra cooked the traditional Iraqi lamb and barley dish called Harissa in a huge pot supported by several cement blocks for the festival of Ashore, one of the most important dates on the Shiite calendar. It takes several hours to cook the dish on a huge fire.

People would spend what they could for these meals. The poor might only serve water or juices, while wealthy people hired specialty chefs for the occasion to perfect the meals. And some cooks offered their services for free, seeking forgiveness or reward, instead.

If you had asked me then if I knew the difference with Islam whether they are Sunni or Shiite, I would not know the difference since at that time they thought about themselves as Muslims. Of course in the south-- where Basra is --the majority were Shea; however, for most of its history, Basra was not Shea, but maintained loyalties to Sunni caliphs.

Chapter 10

Cousins/Arranged Marriages

Inbreeding in theIraqi Culture....
A childhood is what anyone wants to remember of it.
It leaves behind no fossils, except perhaps in fiction.
~Carol Shields~

In an arranged marriage adults rely on their closest family and friends, those who love and know them best, to recommend someone for them to marry based on shared goals, values, experiences and the commitment to make it work.

"Americans just don't understand what a different world Iraq is because of these highly unusual cousin marriages," said Robin Fox of Rutgers University, the author of a widely used anthropology textbook. "Liberal democracy is based on the Western idea of autonomous individuals committed to a public good, but that's not how members of these tight and bounded kin groups see the world. Their world is divided into two groups: kin and strangers."

Several years ago the practice became rare in the West, especially after evidence emerged of genetic risks to offspring, but it has continued in some places, especially the Middle and Far East, which is exceptional, because of the restrictive form it takes. In other societies, a woman typically weds a cousin outside her social group, like a maternal cousin living in a family led by a different patriarch. But in Iraq, the ideal is for the woman to remain within the family by marrying the son of her father's or mother's sibling for one reason only: "trust."

At the local level, the clan traditions and culture provide more support and stability than is true in Western Institutions. That is why divorce rate among married cousins is only 2 percent in Iraq, versus 30-40 percent for other Iraqi couples. But the local ties create national complications. The traditional Iraqis who marry their cousins are very suspicious of outsiders. They are tight knit families who stay within the family. A person growing up with cousins will favor them and trust them. Even when relatives do something wrong, one tends to forgive them, continuing to treat them with respect because they are relatives.

One time after we immigrated to the United States, I was telling my neighbor, who happened to be American born, about a relative of mine who would be married at the end of summer. My neighbor asked me about the process of marriage within my culture. I explained to her that the man interested in a particular girl would ask the parents for the girl's hand. After the parents check on the groom's family, the bride's family would give their consent to allow their daughter to get engaged and then they would go out with each other until they get married. This way each family would have a good idea about the other family.

My neighbor in Michigan (Kay) was shocked to hear about the process of a typical arranged marriage between two families my neighbor, then she said: "You people are amazing. You marry someone you do not know, without dating and your marriage lasts for a lifetime; while in America we date for a long time and live with each other, get married have children and within a couple years we get divorced. This is something I cannot understand."

My answer to my friend was when we are ready to get married we, make a commitment to each other that we will meet half way to accommodate each other knowing that there is no divorce. When individuals plan to get married, there would be screening of each other's families and consideration of any genetic disorders within the other family. Always in our culture when someone wants to get married, both families are screened. Each family must make sure that their own child is making the right choice. Also, it is very important that both families are compatible and well matched in order that marriage will be successful.

Today, some families and friends intervene when they find two people are a good fit to each other. When couples are introduced to each other, both families check on each other to make sure that their children are well protected. Many times my sister or a close friend would say that she saw a girl who would be a good fit for my son. I run the information by my husband and we would make the recommendation to my son to make the move. The next step would be to introduce themselves to each other or exchange phone numbers. There are other ways people are introduced to other with the Internet, since in our culture families know one another. Cousin marriages however, still exist in the Middle East, as well in ethnic cultures in the western countries.

Cousin marriage was once the norm throughout the world, but it became taboo in Europe after a long campaign by the Roman Catholic Church. Theologians like St. Augustine and St. Thomas argued that the practice promoted family loyalties at the expense of universal love and social harmony. Eliminating it was seen as a way to reduce clan warfare and encourage loyalty to larger social institutions—like the church.

An Iraqi/Chaldean community today would make a recommendation to a couple and it sometimes works after they start going out with each other. Although foreign to most of the western world, arranged marriage statistics show that this type of union is often more successful than those we typically see. Common in India, Africa and in some parts of the Middle East, arranged marriages are decided by family members rather than by two people organically.

At the same time divorce rates are anywhere between 40 and 50 percent in Canada and the US. Arranged marriage statistics show us an average divorce rate of 4 percent. This figure is mostly debated because many point out that cultures practicing these types of relationships do not support divorce. The argument is that, if you'll allow someone to arrange your marriage for you, you will also follow the norm and denounce divorce. Similarly, divorce is decidedly more difficult in these countries compared to those in the west.

We hear a lot about young women being killed by their families for not accepting a pre-determined partner. Of course, statistics related to this are not available.

For example, I had a very close friend who was engaged to her first cousin when they were children. It seemed that their parents committed them to each other and that the children would be committed to each other and be faithful to their commitment. Since dating was not permitted, it worked well for the two of them. Even friends and relatives knew about the proposal and the children agreed to it.

As they grew up and they went to different schools and universities, things changed and my girlfriend met someone whom she fell in love with and for a while she was struggling between the two. She started favoring the stranger for her future husband. She said that her cousin's family was different and she did not feel comfortable around them. My friend was confused and needed some direction to be able to face her family.

I was able to advise her to pray for God's guidance and she did. A few weeks later, to her surprise her friend visited her family and asked for her hand in marriage. Her parents agreed and later on she agreed. A month later after the proposal for marriage they were engaged.

I was told that after she was married, her cousin married someone else and both couples are happily married. Her cousin's parents had some hard feelings but they loved both children and forgave the family. We also hear about people in the western world choosing the pre-arranged marriage route out of respect for tradition.

I always said, "If I could go back I would still marry the same man (my husband)." I know not many women feel that way.

Advantages of Cousins/Arranged Marriages

Just why these arranged marriages are so successful (aside from the criticism of divorce that I mentioned earlier) can be a mystery to most. These relationships are chosen by family members seemed to those marriages were built on a set of moral values and beliefs and traditions.

My best friend's Story: After I left Iraq and came to the States, I heard that my best friend who was to marry her cousin was married to someone else, who was living across the street from them. I knew that her cousin's family relocated and she was for a short time away from the picture. I was shocked since her parents had arranged for her to marry her cousin.

Years passed and she ended up in the states, living with her husband very happily. We visited them occasionally to be with them and we took trips together. I learned that her cousin was very interested in her and things were going well between them and his parents were happy, her aunt always introduced her as her son's fiancé.

I became very anxious to hear the detailed story. She said to me, as you knew I was going back and forth to Baghdad and as she said that things were going well until her cousin's became jealous of her because her parents gave her more attention than their own daughter. One day while the two of them were standing in the driveway of the house, her cousin surprised her by bringing to her attention a girl standing by her house about few homes across the street.

My friend said that her cousin said to her "Do you see the girl across the street?" My friend said to her that she never noticed her. Her cousin went on saying to her that her brother is interested in her. My friend was upset the way her cousin tried to tarnish the relationship between her brother and her cousin. My friend did not show anything to her aunt and uncle; however she let her cousin know about the situation and what his sister claimed. His answer was there is nothing between the two of them.

According to my friend, she said with that incident she wanted to stay away from the family. Her uncle and aunt did not know what is going on and why she changed her mind about their son. They carried a grudge towards her mother, thinking that she was the one that kept them away from each other. My girlfriend also informed me that she learned a lot from me especially about faith. She said that she prayed a lot to God to give her the guidance to do the right thing. God heard her prayers and eventually she lived very happily with her husband and her children.

Chapter 11

Iraqi's Focus on Traditions

The Iraqi tradition for preparation for starts the end of October before the cold weather. It starts with "My mother would insist that we clean every window, and I mean every window, inside and out. Clean the couches clean the area rugs and the draperies," In Iraq you can get by with just vacuuming.

My mother was the seamstress for the whole family. She starts a month early and makes dresses and pants and shirts for her sisters, cousins, and for us including night- gowns and pajamas. At that time hand made was preferred and my mother was very creative since her father was a bank manager he ordered sewing catalogs from France for her to work on dressmaking.

Turkish Bath (Hamam)

The history and tradition of the Turkish bath extends hundreds of years as far back as, to a time before Turks had taken over Iraq. However when the Turks arrived Iraq, they brought with them bathing tradition that was a must. The traditions merged, and with the addition of the

Moslem concern for cleanliness and their respect to Koran for the uses of water, there arose an entirely new concept.

Turkish Bath. In time it became an institution, with its system of ineradicable customs. For the Turkish bath was much more than just a place to cleanse the skin. It was intimately bound up with everyday life, a place where people of every rank and station, young and old, rich and poor, townsman or villager, could come freely. Women as well as men made used of the "hamam" as the bath is known in Turkish, although the use was at separate hours.

Since the customs was started for the bride's visit to the hamam; there was a distinctive outfit for cold days, a vest and pair of loose trousers made of fine fabric. This gift from the family of the groom would be worn going to and coming back home from the bath on that special day of the marriage.

Another item the bride needed was a set of towels for the day of the bride's visit to the hamam, that were embroidered in the border with silver thread. In this ornate robe, the bride would be the center of attentions in the bath, and followed by candles and large trays of winter fruits held by maidens and young women. The bride leading the way, the procession would march behind her mother and her future mother-in-law beating a tambourine, around the hamam pool. Young women's voices of the maidens would be heard in song as, candles in hand still burning, they did the circuit of the pool again and again. At some point the bridal veil would be produced to cover the bride's head, and then came the wishing, as unmarried girls tossing coins into the pool in hopes of getting the husband they desired. Today these deeply rooted customs can be observed in the rituals of the Turkish Bath.

It was a place in which to mingle, socialize and gossip. Women would attend to the hamam with their friends and relatives and most of the time the bride to be taken to the public Turkish bath great ceremony. Delicacies are provided to tide the ladies over the hours they would spend lounging in the steam. The young women used this opportunity to show off their lavish embroidered towels with silver or gold threads, and ivory inlaid slippers, not to mention their youthful figures, while older women would spot potential wives for their sons.

Men usually have their own Turkish baths in different locations. Men would discuss the latest court scandal or talk business and politics. Contrary to popular ideas, hamams have always been either permanently designated for one of the sexes, or have a separate schedule for men and women. Both men and women use wooden clogs (slippers) to be able to tolerate the heated floor.

Many hamams were built during the Ottoman era. The Iraqis adopted the style of the idea. The first room encountered is a square court used as a changing area. This leads into a small cooling off section, opening into the hot and steamy, marble clad baths. After being done with bathing the next room where they wrap themselves with towel to dry their hair and body. There were public steam Turkish baths where families would go to enjoy. There were other services offered for adult men in these public steam Turkish baths.

The hamam floor is usually made of stone. It is positioned above the wood or coal furnace that heated the hamam. The bather lies here for a vigorous massage, which involves the removal with a rough cloth glove of a lifetime worth of dead skin. On leaving the hamam, usually people may recover with a cold drink juices or simply stretch out on the reclining couch in the changing area. Hamams have largely gone out of fashion in Turkey today. However, by the time we were born many families adopted the idea and built their own private Turkish baths in their homes.

According to my mother her father when he built their house and for her house and my dad he also built a Turkish bath in his house as he was also remodeling his house exactly the same style of the public Turkish baths and he wanted my mom to use the Turkish bath as a bride and not to go to the public bathrooms.

> *My past is what I've been through, It's not who I am.*
> *It has helped me mold me, but it does not define me.*
> ~ Scarlet Koop, quotes ~

One of the most unforgettable childhood experiences for me is the Turkish Bath that was called the hamam. During those times, my memories take me back when we lived next door to my grandparents. They had a Turkish bath in their house and all the relatives including us went to their house to use the hot steam bath on the weekends. Their house used to be the busiest house on the block.

I remember, beside family, friends and relatives came to enjoy the Turkish bath that was considered of two large rooms, the first one a large room 12 x 12 feet where towels and the clean clothes kept and people take off their clothes and wrap with a towel to enter the second room the same size and when the door open a heavy steam hit your face. However we enjoyed the privacy of having our own private Turkish bath so did our relatives and friends.

These steam bathrooms were to relax after the bath, dry and leave. Taking a Turkish steam bath was considered a luxurious and ritual process. Part of the ritual was a large bowel filled with winter fruits; Oranges, sweet lemons, apples, Pomegranates, and grape fruits. We would go 3-5 people with 2 adults sit on wooden stools. The floor was heated and there were two large hot water containers that get filled by the hot water faucet. Everyone used wooden clogs since the floor was very hot. Both the floor and the water were heated with burning wood fed by the burner located from the outside by the kitchen.

We stayed in the bathroom (Hamam) at least for one hour chatting, pealing and eating citrus fruits. The best part was when the lasting long steam intensifies the fruits. Then the adults will wash our hair and body, and cover us with large towels. We were handed to our mom where she would be waiting at the door to dry us well and put our clean clothes on in the next room.

The dining room that was adjacent to the Turkish bath and the waiting room is the next step to move in to enjoy the warmth of the heater and the smell of hot tea. As we moved to the dining room the cakes, pastries and cookies were served with hot tea. For the adults only, Turkish coffee is served and sometimes a professional lady will read the coffee grinds after the person finishes with drinking the coffee.

When I was about 10 years old, our family was ready to move to a larger house. My parents decided to build a home in a new neighborhood. Our new home was large with our own Turkish bath on the main level, with a heated floor and a regular bath with showers on the upper level, and running hot water.

In the Turkish bath my sisters and I used to stay in the bathroom for few hours and our mother would bring us a bawl of winter fruits such as; (oranges, pomegranates, and apples). And when we were done she would make sure that we are well dried and puts out night gowns and have the tea ready and we get to the family room with the heater on to stay warm.

"I truly miss the coziness of those days."

I pray and hope that our children will teach their children and carry and pass the tradition, although they believe that they are American. However, the cultural differences I would love to see them adopt and carry-on the Chaldean culture. "We enjoy the freedoms and the blessings here in great America but still love our culture and I do the same as my mother and grand mother, and hope to pass it on. In this book culture and tradition is being emphasized and given importance to keep for generations to come.

We have a family recipe for homemade kleicha, the customary holiday sweet cookies stuffed with dates and others with ground walnuts. This is traditionally every home makes them. I remember my grandmother, my aunts, and my mother start kneading the dough the night before and prepare the fillings (walnut mixture and the dates).

Early the next morning before the sun-rise, they will get together at my grand mother's house next door and start making the kleicha, arranging them in large round special trays (45 inch diameter). When they are ready, my grand mother will walk to the baker to come and pick them up to be baked in his large oven. My mother will get her share, and the rest stays with my grandmother, since my mother was the first to get married.

My mother would make us basterma and eggs.

My mother would prepare "Bastirma" early December to be used for the winter. Preparation is time consuming, assist takes a week preparing the casing for stuffing. The meat is made from ground beef meat with garlic and special spices and stuffed with casing like sausages but wider.

The process is to be laid on a hard board lined with newspapers and towels on the newspaper then covered with more towels and another flat wooden board. Finally lots of weight's put, on the top to get the moisture from the meat and kept for 24 hours. Then, tied from both ends and hung on a rope to dry on the outside, while the meat stays red and fresh for the winter season. On Christmas morning, is the first time we start to eat some after the skin is pealed and fried with eggs and added a squeeze of lemon served with freshly baked flat bread and hot tea. It was delicious.

Before Christmas my father would get us stockings that were filled with candy and toys. He hid them for a surprise on Christmas day. He also brought fresh Christmas tree and decorated it. The British planted these pine trees in a sandy area by the oil fields for their own use. Those things were not familiar to the Iraqi culture. However, my father learned many things from his British co-workers.

The day before Christmas my grandmother and aunts prepare the dinner for Christmas called "Pacha" where they work on that al day that consists of lamb stomach where she cut them into 6 inch pieces and stuff them with raw rice and ground lamb meat with spices and saw then like small pockets then she will cooks them on Christmas day with the whole lab head, lamb tongs and lamb legs. We all enjoyed eating them and looked forward to that meal. Almost every Chaldean have the same menu, the same here in the Stated most Chaldean carry that tradition.

Christmas day we wake up with the aroma of the Harrisa

The day before Christmas the Harissa is prepared a mixture of beef chuck roast cut into large pieces and barley with some black pepper and salt in a large pot filled with water and bake over night until the morning. The Harissa to be mixed up by adding more hot water and will be ready for breakfast Christmas Day.

When it is the time to get ready to attend the church for the midnight Mass we would go home with our mother and dress us with a new dress and new shoes. The mass was very long and mot of the time we would fall asleep. Some of the Christmas traditions they found here were familiar—Iraqi Christians, like their American counterparts, put up Christmas trees and attend midnight Mass on Christmas Eve. "We love the music and the singing; that's something we had Christmas song in Iraq in Arabic and French. After the midnight mass we go home to sleep.

We would be in a hurry to get our gifts. Chaldean children are given small amounts of money, called (eidania), by their parents or grandparents, sometimes slipped under their pillows on Christmas night.

You find people are greeting each other; "edi moubarak" or "eid brekha", meaning "blessed feast," the second one is in dialect of Aramaic language, a direct descendent of the language used by Jesus Christ.

But the holiday was more meaningful, simpler and not as commercialized in Iraq, as I recall. Because Chaldeans are a minority in an Iraq, there are few public expressions of the holiday there. And to the Chaldeans, Christmas is of less importance than Easter.

But Santa Claus and lavish gift exchanges were not known then. I still remember that as a child, "" my mother wouldn't let us touch the (Christmas cookies) kleicha until Christmas Day," "She said the Lord hadn't blessed it yet" so she put it on top of the closet. It was emphasized that Christmas is about Jesus and the Nativity.

Kleicha- Christmas Cookies

The most important feature of a Chaldean Christmas is the visitation of relatives. In Iraq, the visits began immediately after midnight Mass, I recalled, with families calling on relatives until the late hours of the morning.

Chaldeans would then arise later that morning and begin more visiting—grandparents, in-laws, aunts, uncles, and even distant cousins. And then those relatives would return the visits. And the obligations don't end on Christmas day.

"If you can't see someone the next day, or even in the next few weeks, you are expected to greet them with a Christmas greeting when you do see them. I worry that within time and after several generations our grandchildren will forget the old

This tea glasses are used only for tea with no milk

cups and coffee server

Some women were professional
fortune cup reader

Kleicha-Christmas Cookies stuffed with walnuts and dated

Chapter 12

A Tour North of Basra and south of Baghdad

The wetland region where the Tigris and Euphrates rivers split into meandering ribbons and lakes before flowing into the Persian Gulf has been home to human communities for five millennia. Since it was mentioned in the Bible several times, particularly in these locations is the Garden of Eden positioned near the two rivers (Genesis chapter 2, verse 14).

The Marshes is natural lagoons 5000 years BC, defined where nature seems to preserve its virgin aspect. Miles and miles of water, with an endless variety of birds, fish, plants and reeds, dotted as far as the eye can see with huts, each a little island has its own boundaries.

Apart from the townsmen, here you see farmers from the rich Mesopotamian vicinity, weather-beaten men in black and brown cloaks; Marsh Arabs, similarly dressed but their hands and feet are bigger and hornier from constant contact with canoe-paddles, the decks of boats and slashing, stabbing reed-stubble; men from the direction of Kuwait in red and white check head-cloths, clicking beads, eyes half-buried in skin wrinkled from squinting into the sun. In the hot weather, sit in the doorway to catch what breeze you can.

Abraham Stopped here

Abraham's home was in a city called Ur (in modern day Iraq). Here God first appeared to him. After miles and miles of a barren landscape comes a small pond surrounded with tall reeds and hundreds of date palms. Minnows swim. Birds and bullfrogs abound.

Legend holds that Abraham, patriarch to the Jewish, Christian and Muslim peoples, stopped at an oasis with his family while traveling from Mesopotamia to Canaan. A small village grew up at the oasis in the 20th century.

Abraham's Death

At the age of 175 years, 100 years after he had first entered the land of Abraham died and was buried in the old family burial cave. The history of Abraham made a wide and deep impression on the ancient world, and references to it religious traditions of almost all Eastern nations. He was called "the friend of God", "faithful Abraham". He is the father of the three religions Judaism, Christianity, and Islam.

"Author: Matthew G. Easton, edited for accuracy by Paul S. Taylor.

Visiting Al-Ahwar

These wetlands north of Basra were called Al-ahwar located close to the Tigris and Euphrates Rivers merge, you would think you are in haven. The once fertile land, some believe to have been the biblical Garden of Eden and Abraham stopped there while traveling. It was also called marsh Arab. This community lived there farming and making their own living and selling fresh fish and milk products.

I was 11 years old the first time I saw Alahwar (Marshes), just east of the Baghdad-Basra highway. For miles, thousands of reed huts stood on earth and papyrus islands, each inhabited by the descendants of the ancient Sumerians, a time warp of simplicity which, according to old Arabic scripts, may have begun with a devastating flood around AD620.

It was known that more than 5,000 years, the people there maintained an ancient lifestyle in one of the most fertile and flourishing environments on earth. They lived in homes made of reed floating on shallow waters, traveling from village to village in small boats, fishing and growing rice among the water buffalo.

It has been known, those marsh Arabs, who numbered about a half a million people in the 1950's, have decreased to as few as 20,000 today, according to the United Nations.

The southern end of the river constitutes the border between Iraq and Iran down to the mouth of the river as it discharges into the Persian Gulf. It was thought that the waterway formed relatively recently in geologic time, with the Tigris and Euphrates originally emptying into the Persian Gulf through a channel further to the west.

According to the history of this area, after the end of the war, the UK was given responsibility, later mandated by United Nations Security Council Resolution 1723, to patrol the waterway and the area of the Persian Gulf surrounding the river mouth. They are tasked to make sure that ships in the area are not being used to transport arms into Iraq. The British Army also trained Iraqi naval units to take over the responsibility of guarding their waterways.

Marsh Region

Looking back, it was a blessing to see the Marsh Arabs that is called (Al ahwar) this is a unique community that has its own culture. This society was on the way to Baghdad as soon as you leave Basra. The Garden of Eden, is believed to be located near the Marsh Arabs.

The region of Shatt al-Arab is considered to be the largest date palm forest in the world. In the mid-1950s, the region counted some 18–20 million date palms or a fifth of the world's 90 million palm trees.

The Iranian city of Abadan and the Iraqi city and major port of Basra are situated along this river. Control of the waterway and its use as a border have been a source of contention between the predecessors of the Iranian and Iraqi states since a peace treaty signed in 1639 between the Persian and the Ottoman Empires, which divided the territory according to tribal customs and loyalties, without attempting a rigorous land survey. The tribes on both sides of the lower waterway, however, are Marsh Arabs, and the Ottoman Empire claimed to represent them.

The main thrust of the military movement on the ground was across the waterway, which was the stage for most of the military battles between the two armies. The waterway was Iraq's only outlet to the Persian Gulf, and thus, its shipping lanes were greatly affected by continuous Iranian attacks. The Al-Faw peninsula was captured by the Iranians in 1987, Iraq's shipping activities virtually came to a halt and had to be diverted to other Arab ports, such as Kuwait and even Aqaba, Jordan.

Following the end of the war, the UK was given responsibility, subsequently mandated by United Nations Security Council Resolution 1723, to patrol the waterway and the area of the Persian Gulf surrounding the river mouth. They are tasked to make sure that ships in the area are not being used to transport munitions into Iraq. British forces have also trained Iraqi naval units to take over the responsibility of guarding their waterways.

(Taken from Wikipedia, the free encyclopedia)

(Taken from Wikipedia, the free encyclopedia)
Marsh Region

Chapter 13

Who are the Chaldeans?

As a descendant of one of the earliest Iraqi Christians I try each year to follow the tradition to celebrate Chaldean Christmas. The Chaldeans speak Aramiac, also spoken by Jesus Christ. The Chaldeans represent most of the 5 percent of Iraqis who profess Christianity and have survived far worse.

The Chaldean people, lived mostly in northern Iraq and of trace their ancestry, back 8,000 years. They are mentioned in the Book of Genesis. Hammurabi was Chaldean, as was Nebuchadnezzar. Chaldeans began converting to Christianity before the middle of the first century. They're now aligned with the Roman Catholic Church.

It was great especially during the Holidays. My grandfather was the senior Deacon in the church and we were to be at our best in church. The church was about 300 feet away from our homes. Since we attended the French Nuns School, we knew that we were Chaldeans because we attended the Chaldean Church.

My parents and grandparents were never heard speaking Chaldean. We knew that we were Chaldeans living in Iraq that became an Arab Country. Then later we understood and learned from the history classes that the Chaldeans were the original inhabitant of what is called Iraq. Chaldeans celebrated each year a Chaldean Christmas as they were accustomed to it for generations.

The ritual visits to relatives are continues today. The midday Christmas feast this year may be at P.F. Chang's. Even the family recipe for homemade *koleicha*, the customary sweet cakes, has been adapted to life along the US traditions. My mother wouldn't let us touch the *koleicha* until Christmas Day. My mother said. "The Lord hadn't blessed it yet, so she put it on top of the refrigerator."

The Chaldeans, who represent most of the 50 percent of Iraqis who profess Christianity, have survived far worse from Iraqi's invaders.

The Chaldean people, who now live mostly in northern Iraq, trace their ancestry back 8,000 years. They are mentioned in the Book of Genesis. Hammurabi was Chaldean, as was Nebuchadnezzar. Chaldeans began converting to Christianity before the middle of the first century. They're now aligned with the Roman Catholic Church. Chaldeans speak a dialect of Aramaic, a direct descendant of the language used by Jesus Christ.

According to the Chaldeansonline.net. Estimated over 250,000 Chaldeans who live in the U.S. according to the Web site Chaldeansonline.net. Most have settled in Detroit, Phoenix, Chicago or southern California, where most are somehow Some of the Christmas traditions they found here were familiar – Today, Iraqi Christians, like their American counterparts, put up Christmas trees and attend midnight Mass on Christmas Eve.

Chaldean children have been adapted to the American tradition celebrating Christmas. Our first years we continued the Iraqi traditions by giving children small amounts of money, called *eidania*, or slipped under their pillows on Christmas night.

Later on Santa Claus and lavish gift exchanges were practiced for the children to feel as the other American children. We have adapted to the American Christmas. Gifts for children sit under the family tree, wrapped in paper decorated with snowmen. "We do give gifts,". "But we try to emphasize that Christmas is about Jesus and the Nativity."

The most important feature of a Chaldean Christmas is the visitation of relatives. In Iraq, the visits began immediately after midnight Mass, Mrs. celebrating with families calling on relatives until the wee hours of the morning.

Chaldeans would then arise later that morning and begin more visiting – grandparents, in-laws, aunts, uncles, also, distant cousins. And then those relatives would return the visits.

Today, our family members expected to gather in their parents and grand-parents homes in Michigan, and a phone will be passed from relative to relative calling other relatives who are celebrating with their own children.

I insist on keeping the tradition and do not wish the children and the grandchildren to forget our old traditions. We enjoy the freedoms and the blessings here in America and I admire many of the American Christmas traditions.

In the Cradle of Civilization

The Tigris and Euphrates Rivers divides Baghdad. Christian enjoyed a high measure of religious freedom often found in the city. The Chaldean Church of the East was founded by the Apostle St. Thomas. He spread Christianity to Mesopotamia and India's other churches.

In Baghdad was a large population of Christian churches of various denominations.

So who are the Chaldean Iraqis?

According to what I recall from the history books:

1. Thousand years ago, they invented and irrigated farming.
2. They invented writing.
3. They were the ones who time and including the 60 minutes 1 hour.
4. They founded modern mathematics.
5. In the Code of Hammurabi the first legal system to protects the weak widow and the orphan.
6. They invented artificial building materials, used to construct high-rise towers.
7. They were the first people to build cities and live in them.
8. Because they used horses they became great horse breeders.
9. The Iraqi Museum in Baghdad displayed the most exceptional stone, metal and clay creations. Some of them are more than 7,000 years old.
10. They invented the wheel.
11. The first school for Astronomy Science was recognized by Iraqis where the wise men became wise and knew how to follow the star.

12. For the first 1,200 years of its existence, Baghdad was regarded as one of the most refined civilized and festive cities in the world.
13. Abraham, the father of Judaism, was from Iraq.
14. Abraham, the father of Islam, was from Iraq.
15. Abraham, the father and "model" of Christian faith, was from Iraq

Jews and Assyrian Christians forced migrations between 1843 and the 21st century during the Ottoman occupation of the Middle East.

An important study from an analytical and comparative point of view, comparing the Chaldean/Assyrian Christians experience with the experience of the Kurdish Jews who had been dwelling in Kurdistan for two thousands years or so, but were forced to migrate the land to Israel in the early 1950s.

Kurdistan Jews were forced to migrate as a result of the Arab-Israeli war, as a result of the increasing hostility and acts of violence against Jews in Iraq and Kurdish towns and as a result of a new situation that had been built up during the 1940s in Iraq and Kurdistan in which the Jews to live in comfort and relative tolerance with their Arab and Muslim neighbors, as they did for many years, practically came to an end.

At the end, the Jews of Kurdistan had to leave their Kurdish habitat and migrate into Israel. The Assyrian Christians on the other hand, came to similar conclusion but migrated in stages following each and every eruption of a political crisis with the regime in which boundaries they lived or following each conflict with their Muslim, Turkish, Arabs or Kurdish neighbors. Consequently, indeed there is still a small and fragile community of Chaldean/Assyrians in Iraq; however, millions of Assyrian Christians live today in exile in prosperous communities in the west.

Iraqi/Chaldean Cuisine was influenced by the neighboring countries in particular Persia and Turkey occupied Iraq. The Iraqi community, were affected by these countries not only with the different food but also they adopted some of the languages and added to the Arabic Language.

The importance of culinary art for the Ottoman culture:

Iraqi Chaldeans in that period of occupation of The Ottoman were introduced to different taste and flavors adding cardamom and Saffron to the food to enhance long run improved the taste by adding more Saffron and cardamom to the food to improve and enhance the flavor. Iraqi's improved cuisine of the however not all Iraqi's use these spices.

You would find the Iraqi adapted to certain flavors according to the cities they lived in if it was in the north or the south depends on the location. For instance we lived in Basra was neighboring Iran. Basra cooking is famous to season the food with Cardamom and Saffron since Iran is famous with these particular spices.

Basra's location by the Arabian Golf, we had the large boats stop in the port of Basra to load and unload merchandize coming from the east and west. Citizens of Basra are known for eating spicy food that came from India.

Iraqi Chaldeans had different cuisine since they were farmers in the north of Iraq where they felt safe and would farm wheat, barley and vegetables and fruits for every season. They used to bake their own bread that was the most delicious, fresh and baked daily.

Chapter 14

*"One day your life will flash before your eyes. Make sure
it's worth watching."* --
~Anonymous~

4th. Of July Revolution (1958)

We woke up that day in Basra with the radio station from Baghdad announcing that the army had taken over the country and they are under control. There were all kinds of announcements such as enforcing curfew and any one found on the streets will be shot.

We later heard that in the early hours of 14 July, a group of high army personnel took over the government and seized control of Baghdad's broadcasting station (which was to become his Head Quarters.) and broadcast and they promised of a future election for a new president.

That day, the army Jeeps and some army on foot imposed a curfew all over the cities of Iraq' including Basra to enforce security and protection to the citizens. However, it was moments of insecure feelings and we were nervous and having mixed feelings about the situation and what is going to happen next.

The uprising situation remained that way for three to four days with curfews enforced and the condition settled down and people resumed their daily routine. It was summer vacation for us in school so we did not miss anything.

The revolution aftermath

The first Iraqi revolution erupted against the Monarchy rulings. It was a whole different story in Baghdad, on the morning of July 14, 1958. The mutineers from the armed forces had broken into the royal palace. The young king, Faisal II, a harmless young man 23 years of age, and his grandmother and a devoted aunt, along with all the other members of the royal household, were assembled in the courtyard and gunned down.

Two weeks after the revolution, a temporary constitution was announced, pending to develop a permanent law to be declared officially. Several revolutions occurred in the country for a period of few years, when the country had control by the army. Most of the activities were happening in Baghdad.

With Basra being far from the capital with no television broadcast at the time, it was hard to estimate the situation in Baghdad. However, when a revolution was planned the boarders were secured the citizens for their safety. I don't remember feeling any danger. However, we were wandering what is going to happen next.

My parents thought that the situation is going to affect the foreign establishments and since our school was owned and run by French nuns they might have to leave the country. We were afraid to talk on the phones it might be tapped. We were unable to visit our neighbors to check on the situation on the outside.

We later heard about the killings and some people were jailed for resisting the new governmental régime. We knew that the new administration was going to be rough and strong, since it was associated with the army. Thinking about the situation, I realize that the Iraqi citizens were resilient, and were able to take on to any situation.

Although Basra was far from Baghdad, the peace and the borders were controlled by the army and there was curfew to limit and control trouble makers on the streets for few weeks. Banks, offices and schools were closed. People went shopping in the mornings for a few hours when the curfew time was off.

For us children it was fun. Although it was during the summer vacation, things were unpredictable. It took 2-3 weeks for the country to be stabilized. What a difference between then, and the American invasion of Iraq, in 2003.

I loved my family and they loved me, and wanted to protect me with my older sister, and at the same time, get the best education possible in a safe environment. Growing up, I came to know that my mother's aunt (Aunty Mary) was also in India/Calcutta, with her blind father who was a very smart man. He took her and his young son (3) years old and his other stepdaughter my grand mother.

At the time my, grand mother (Mama Josa) went with them and she was pregnant with my mother. My mother was born in India. Knowing this background about my family I know that was the best arrangement for my schooling. I do not regret it was as it a great experience.

During this time my parents made their decision to send me to India to join my older sister. I had no choice I believed that my parents know best. The plan was to travel with my mother's aunt, who referred education in India. Aunty Mary immediately began the course of action applying for the passports, visas and her vacation from work. She prepared to leave by a cruise ship.

My parents and Aunty Mary were making arrangements with the school in India for me to start in September. Aunt Mary wanted to take me herself so, she arranged a trip on the Ship Dara that sails from Basra to Bombay.

Chapter 15

---

*"Memory is a way of holding on to the things you love,
the things you are, the things you never want to lose."
~Kevin Arnold~*

Going to India

Aunty Mary, my mother's aunt who had her education in Calcutta India, wanted to take me by ship to Panchgani via Poona/Bombay. She worked on the arrangements for the school, visa and the boat tickets to travel with me to enter the boarding school

On the planned day we arrived at the ship and after she presented the passports and the visas we were taken to our cabin. The cabin was a good size and the family came on board to make sure that everything is going well. Then the family said their goodbye, my aunt completed the paperwork. We went to our cabin when the busboy came with the dinner - fish patties. The Gulf's fish is known as the best seafood in the world, it was great.

As we finished eating, the captain of the ship knocked on the door and came in to let us know that there were some mistakes in my papers, and we cannot sail with them. The papers need to be taken to the passport department to be corrected since I was underage. The passport must have a guardianship from my parents in order for my aunt to accompany me to school.

We had no choice but to leave the ship. Thank God my parents and the rest of the family were waiting by the harbor for the ship to sail. They were surprised to see us back. Aunty Mary had the biggest disappointment on her face. She said to me that this was an opportunity for her to visit India again. She was right, she never had the chance to visit India again.

My parents and Aunty Mary started working on my traveling papers making sure that everything is in order. My dad had an Indian business acquaintance was taking his family to India for summer vacation traveling by the cruise ship. My dad asked Mr. Patel if they do not mind taking me to India with them since they had girls my age. The Patel family welcomed me to go with them and the girls were delightful.

On the day of departure, my parents were with me at the time of the ship to embark. They were busy finalizing all the legal travel documents including the passport. My family came onboard to check my cabin and talked to their friends (my chaperones) making sure that one of the family's daughters who is the same age as me will stay in my room to keep me company.

Being sheltered all my life in a catholic school with French nuns, I was naïve to what is happening, just trusting that my parents made the right and the best arrangement for me to travel with a family we did not know well. I guess in those times, people were honest and loving.

The ship left the port of Basra on a beautiful early September day, 1958, leaving Iraq by myself to sail a large passenger cruise ship. All I know at this time is that my older sister, who was already in a boarding school in India, will be meeting me on my arrival to Bombay.

The Persian Gulf, British India steadily expanded its services, both in capacity and in the ports of call serviced. The original trade, however, focused on the Bombay to Basra axis and this was continued until the late sixties, when port congestion along the Tigris-Euphrates halted British India services at Kuwait. The ship sailed from Basra, estimated a 10-day trip with daily stops along the way at different ports. The main ports of call continued to be Kuwait, Bahrain, Doha, Dubai, Muscat and Karachi with several smaller ports called at sporadically.

We did not get off the ship. I guess the family did not want to take a risk to go down with us the children. We were able to see passengers embark and disembark the ship. The weather was pleasant and changing from one country to another. We were introduced to other Iraqi people traveling to other countries.

The trip was great I had a great time with the Patel Family. Time went too fast and we arrived in Bombay with my sister waiting for our arrival at the docks. I noticed also the school Principal Sister Cecilia Joseph and my sister's friend, who lived as our neighbor and was also Iraqi from Basra.

After I received my luggage and I was telling them about my trip that I was comfortable and the Patel's family were very helpful and I enjoyed their company. Then we were on our way to the convent where we will stay few days before we leave to Panchgani. I was happy to see someone familiar, my sister. After I was introduced to Mother Cecilia Joseph. She was the most affectionate, warm and loving nun you could ever meet. The minute she received me landing from the ship, she gave me the biggest hug you could imagine, with a big smile she welcomed me.

After we got to St. Joseph orphanage in Bombay (their other affiliated convent), we were guided to our bedroom to rest and we were offered to drink chai (tea). We were reconnecting since my sister left Basra year ago. Then I learned that we are going to the movies to see the Ten Commandments that will be showing for the first time in India. We also knew that we would never be able to see it in Iraq since it was banned at all of the Arab countries. Since the actors and the producer were Israeli. It was a great movie and we enjoyed it. Moreover, this was the first time for us to see a movie with cinemascope.

We stayed in Bombay for four days for sight seeing. At that time we were not interested in shopping. We visited the Zoo that had many animals we have not seen. That was the first time for me to visit any zoo. As we returned to the convent at the end of the day, we were very tired and went to sleep.

We slept in a large room where the teachers slept. They had extra beds for visitors. We had a good night sleep. The teachers were interested to know us since they never had students from the Middle East, especially from Basra.

There had all kind of questions and they were fascinated about the Iraqi/Chaldean culture after they came to know the connection of Christianity and the Chaldeans since these teachers themselves were Christians. One of the teachers was aware of the Chaldeans since there were a large community in Malabar (North of Bombay) were of the descendents of the Chaldean who came with St. Thomas on his journey spreading the Christian religion.

On the fourth day we were ready to go to Panchgani. My sister and her friend were filling me in on the school I am about to enter. They were involved with the business program that they are attending business and office training with typing and English Language. I was going to be attending a traditional grade school. We started to pack to get back to school.

Mother Cecilia Joseph, an Irish nun was the most warm and loving nun you could ever meet. She had the most heartfelt hugs you ever can have. Mother Cecilia Joseph guided the three of us toward the train station to take the train to Poona.

Poona

I will never forget the long bus trip to Poona, during which we passed through numerous Indian villages. Each time the bus stopped all the European passengers, including myself, were surrounded by Indian beggars, many of them crippled. The sight of these maimed and injured children and emaciated, seriously crippled adults, was very distressing to us. Some people gave a coin just to be relieved of this disturbing company.

However, frequently one satisfied beggar attracted many others to a benefactor in the bus. It was impossible to help all those who besieged us. It was claimed that many poverty-stricken parents deliberately crippled their children in infancy to ensure they would be beggars for life and provide them with a constant source of income. I felt much relieved each time the bus moved on.

Poona was, at one time, the foundation of the great Maratha Empire and is closely associated with the military. As the train approached Poona, we picked our luggage heading to the bus station to connect with the bus that would take us to Panchgani.

Panchgani

It was the end of the summer as autumn' begin. We felt the change of the temperature falling and the cool air hit our faces. It felt good as we approached the mountain area. We arrived to Panchgani in two hours and the ride was pleasant. About 100 km from Puna is the place that was discovered by the British to have a suitable place where the wives and children of the officers could live permanently without pining to go back to England. Since then, it has been considered an educational centre and was affiliated with Cambridge/England.

Each place has something unique to offer. Panchgani had a pleasant cool weather, surrounded with trees that had the fruits seen on the trees. I pointed at the mango trees and I asked "what are those on these trees?" Mother Cecilia answered: "those are mango trees and the mangos are not ripe yet". Since I love fruits to get them directly from the tree, I assured myself that I would wait for them to get ripe. A particular sweet smell, the way the breeze hums when it flirts with the trees or maybe the taste of water or may be even a falling of emotion that you associate with the hills when you go there for the first time.

One of the first things you notice as you drive into Panchgani are the number of schools that are tucked away inside the curves and turns of the hill station. In fact, you might know that Panchgani is famous for its numerous boarding schools. Many prefer to get a glimpse of the sweet blend or romance that fits all around. One must see chart or marked Sidney point is another favorite sightseer area. Then there is the Krishna Valley and near blue waters of the Dhom dam. Tableland is the Panchgani Pleasure and a hotspot that you cannot miss. It is one of the largest Table Lands in the continent and is famous for film shootings.

Panchgani was discovered the by the British who were looking for a secluded area near Puna that could fit for an educational-town. Since Bombay during the war had a lot of diseases so the British were in afraid that their children getting sick if they stayed in the city of Bombay. Panchgany was a very suitable village that provided a clean, disease-free setting for the youth.

Panchgani's crisp mountain air and friendly people were considered ideally suitable for such a village. Boarding schools were soon set up for these privileged children of the British in Western India. It was not long before the wealthy merchant princes of Bombay began seeking admission in these schools for their own children

My favorite nun, I cannot remember her name, she was German with a heavy accent. I was one of her favorite students. One day while I was picking my clothes from the main locker, she started asking me questions about my plans for the future. I remember I said that I will be someone important but did not get into details. She reminded me that I am different from all the other Iraqi students and encouraged me to try and finish college. Most of my teachers supported me during my schooling in India.

The boarding school was a very good experience for me. My friends asked for advice were always approaching me on different issues. I remember a close friend of mine who had a personal problem and after a few days of talking it over, we were able to get all the differences resolved. This incident gave me the image of a "helper", which led other students to ask for advice and I was always ready to help.

A normal weekday in School

Our school days started at 7.00 a.m. followed by the morning prayers in the dormitories, each supervised by an older student. After we showered, dressed and we were made our own beds before hurrying to breakfast that usually consisted of porridge and two slices of bread, or with butter and fruit homemade jam. On Sundays we had eggs and sausages or bacon.

After breakfast we walked to the school chapel there we said our morning prayers. Morning prayers were assigned from the bible. We sang a couple of hymns from the prayer book and recited selected short prayers. After we were done with the morning prayers, special school notices were read out at the end.

We had one morning recess and another before lunch. Normally lunch was curry and rice that was my favorite of curry and rice, Dahl and two slices of bread. Sometimes we took an afternoon nap. Followed by afternoon tea the English way. We had two classes where the school schedule is done. After school, we went for a walk or played sports either Hockey or volleyball at the tablelands. Usually we walked there in pairs, supervised by a teacher, carrying our own hockey sticks. We always looked forward to these outings.

Our routine change during the monsoon season we could only play indoor basketball in our gymnasium. Sometimes we took different route walking in the rain, dressed in raincoats. The Monsoon season was from mid-May to September heavy rain continued without a break. Gloomy cloudy skies continued till October, when blue skies changes and it is the beginning of the dry season with sunny skies.

The school syllabus prepared us for the junior and senior Cambridge external examinations, which were set and marked in England. At first I was placed in the eighth class, because I had already had two years of secondary education in French/Arabic in Iraq. However, my knowledge of English was meager. I had learned it only as a second language and had had no opportunity to speak it.

As for the algebra and geometry I managed and eventually they decided to place me in that class, to ensure a thorough grounding in mathematics. I was then also transferred to a junior dormitory and a junior class, where the girls were several years younger than I was.

I felt the gap between myself and the other students. I was already 14 years old, bigger and also more physically mature than the students with whom I shared my classes with them. Additionally, at St. Joseph School I had been a couple years older than my classmates, so I was very uncomfortable with the arrangement. I progressed quickly however, to become more able to communicate with my peers. By the following year, I was fluent In English with a British accent, and I was able to skip a grade.

Nevertheless, I found myself involved in every trivial relationship or challenge of the students. Soon I was known as the "problem solver". The most important issue was not the advice, but that I was reliable and able to keep their secrets. I believe this experience had a great effect in shaping my personality and my love to help other people. After three years in India I went home for summer vacation and refused to go back.

A strong guidance I felt and feel which grew to a trust in myself, and as the trust increased, my power to achieve my goals increased also. There were several attempts for me to achieve my goals earlier but it seemed that an outside force was blocking my dreams. It felt what I wanted was not meant to be.

There was a lot of uncertainty concerning peace, and what is going to happen to the French nuns school was the biggest concern of my parents. They looked for alternatives and there were discussions with other family members. Since my older sister was already in India and was happy in the school she was attending, my parents thought that will be a good idea for me to join my sister in India.

The monsoon season around in the spring the tablelands seemed to carpeted with and wild violets. This was a splendid sight to you ever see. The hills in Panchgani were composed of very hard rocks and caves.

The Roman Catholic Girls,' St. Joseph's Convent High School that I attended was a missionary school catered for a mixture of Indian, European and Anglo-Indian pupils, mainly Anglo-Indians and British. Christian missionaries first ran the early schools and education was imparted with an emphasis on Christian values and moral codes under our Principal Mother Cecilia Joseph.

Mostly Irish, Germen and some Indian nuns had staffed St. Joseph's Boarding school. There was a small farm adjacent to the convent. The nuns were very busy as they provided some revenue for the care of these abandoned children in the orphanage in Bombay.

The nuns also grew their own vegetables, and some fruit such as oranges, lemons, grapefruit and mangoes. They also kept cows for milk and Angora rabbits for their fiber. Fowls provided eggs; ducks and geese were reared for poultry meat, and pigs for the holidays to be cooked with curry. This enterprise made it possible for the school to meet its charitable obligations in addition to admitting fee-paying students. Many Polish girls benefitted from the education received at the St. Joseph's High School, where they became fluent in English.

Famous roasted gram in its three varieties (plain, lemon, spiced), do rounds in the market, and during your walk to visit. The Tableland is where the "Shooting point" for a number of Hindi films had been come to The Plateau. I found it hard believe that this place has an edge - a steep fall into the Krishna valley from all sides. An endless ocean of land, barren except when it rains, where it turns into a lush green carpet overloaded with charming daisies and other flora and a lake fills up in the middle turning it into wonderland.

It was very scary for me to go through the peer down a steep slope and take in the charming scenery of the Krishna River flowing among agrarian greens and browns, and watch a paraglide sail over the panorama airborne. The first time I visited the Krishna River, it was scary for someone like me, coming from Basra that had flat leveled land.

Down below you see roofs of schools, British bungalows and school-bys and girls coming up for a game of football. Panchgani has a rich collection of historic buildings. Some bungalows date from the turn of the 19th century - many belong to the early part of the 20th century and are charming - verandahs, sloping roofs painted bright red.

Later, I enrolled in the hockey team. I enjoyed playing hockey on the tableland. It was a rough game for girls. I remember I was always hit with the flat ball on my ankle. But it was fun. I enjoyed sports; I enrolled in the basketball team too.

With Panchgani having elite boarding schools like St. Peters a boarding school for boys and St. Joseph's Convent, the prestigious all-girls' institute, where such starry boarders as many famous actresses have studied, there is bound to be landscape. Here is a jolly discussion that took place in Panchgani.

This occurred during tea party, incidentally among the Principals of the Panchgani schools. The British who were worried about their families to find a suitable place where the wives and children of the officers of the Company could reside, instead of going back to England. Pachgani was founded in 1853. Since then, Panchgani has been an educational Center and hill resort.

The view from Tableland, a flat mountain peak measuring about one square kilometer, exposes the mysterious valleys and the miniature looking plains on all sides. The Caves, fort, Municipal Garden and the Children's park add to Panchgani's unending beauty.

The walkways, thickly canopied by lush trees and vegetation, offer many delights

Visitors can select a horse from one of the numerous stables at the resort and canter along uncharted routes through hidden lover's lanes, to the caves or while a way their time at the bazaar. Also available are the famous, pith flowers, exclusive saris shawls, readymade garments, eye-catching decorative items, leather goods and tribal trinkets.

During the monsoon season we could only play indoor basketball in our gymnasium, but ventured out daily for long walks in the rain, dressed in raincoats (mackintoshes) and gumboots (Wellingtons). From mid-May to September heavy rain continued without a break. The gloomy cloudy skies continued till October, when blue skies changes and welcomes the beginning of the dry spells of the retreating monsoon rain.

I felt the gap between myself and the other students. I was already 14 years old, bigger and also more physically mature than the students with whom I shared my classes with them. Additionally, at St. Joseph School I had been a couple years older than my classmates, so I was very uncomfortable with the arrangement. I progressed quickly however, to become more able to communicate with my peers. By the following year, I was fluent In English with a British accent, and I was able to skip a grade.

The nuns arranged a monthly, a dancing party and invited St. Mary's boys school to attend the Gala and enjoy the music and dancing with the nuns, and the teachers to be the chaperons for the event. A Scottish pipe band, to played which we had never heard before and there was colorful tartan robes, rhythmical marching and the sound of the bagpipes, when St. Mary's boys preformed before the gala started.

Prior to the gala, we were instructed to behave like young ladies and not to encourage the boy that we were dancing with to not get too close, other wise we will be pulled out of the ballroom. Sometimes we girls danced with each other to avoid problems with aggressive boys. It was an unforgettable experience. My sister and I were also fascinated by the Panchgani bazaars, which we were able to explore during the long, winter holidays. The school was closed during the holiday, starting in December to February, during the very hot, dry season in India.

*{Rita Farria was Miss World Pageant in 1962, and was about to graduate from high school when I entered the school 7th grade. I remember her being a beautiful girl.}

Transferring to Bombay

After a year, Mother Cecilia Joseph was transferred to Bombay. The new Principal, who was an Indian nun, was just the opposite of Mother Cecilia. Most of the foreigner students were complaining and did not want to have the new principal. She was very strict, and she was bitter and never smiled.

During the Christmas Holiday, my sister and I wrote to our parents to be spend the holidays with Mother Cecilia. We went to Bombay to visit and remained there, in a small room used by one of the nuns on the staff and we dined with the teachers. At that time nuns did not dine with outsiders, in keeping with their convent rules and very strict discipline. It was a great experience.

During our stay in Bombay, I had abdominal pain. I was seen by the St. Joseph's doctor and was recommended to get to the hospital. I was scheduled for appendix removal surgery. I was glad that my sister was there as she is family. The following week, Mother Cecilia arranged for the surgery in one of the local hospitals and also arranged one of her staff nurse to stay with me in the hospital.

On the day of surgery I was on time at the hospital that was built by the British. The surgery preparation and recovery took 2 hours. After I woke up, I found myself in the hospital room and my private nurse was with me. I stayed in the hospital for 3 days.

The day of discharge I left the hospital and I remember that I was holding my stomach all the time. As a matter of fact, Mother Cecilia asked me one day "how come you are holding your stomach, is everything is ok? I used to say to her,"it feels something is moving in my stomach".

It was not funny, but I found out after forty years when I had my colonoscopy test. The doctor asked me, "what was the cut on my stomach? My answer was that, "I had my appendix removed in India." The doctor saw on my face I was puzzled. He then explained that my colon has been removed from where it was supposed to be and never put back in the same order after the surgery. I said to him "no wonder I always feel my stomach stuffed after I eat small meal".

While, I was in Bombay, the premiere for the movie Ben-Hur came to town and I was asked to help to be with other students from St. Mary's and St. Joseph Schools in Bombay to distribute the Program Booklets the day of the film Ben-Hur's Grand opening.

After my sister left India, I started going to school at St. Mary's Catholic that was close to the convent, within walking distance. I did well until the end of the year. My parents wanted me to go home for the summer vacation. I was excited to go home. I was ready to visit home. I missed my family --- Somehow I felt lost.

I was busy shopping. My mother sent me a list to get things from India and I started making my dresses since they have the best tailors to fit well. I stayed one month extra to complete my shopping. It was a fun time I went a lot to the movies and visited tourist areas and famous attractions.

Although Mother Cecilia tried her best to make me happy and accommodate my needs, I still felt lonely. I liked the idea to go back home. Mother Cecilia made arrangements for my travel with another Iraqi student. She was coming from St. Joseph Convent, Pachgani in order to travel together since we were both under age, lived in the same city of Basra, and would land at the same airport.

Mother Cecilia took us to the airport to take the plane that had one stop at Karachi in Pakistan. Mother Cecilia made all the arrangements at the airport and made sure that we will be taken care of by the airhostess be in-charge to make sure that she will hand us to our parents.

Upon our arrival to Karachi, the plane was expected to stop for one hour to fuel and pick up more passengers. Karachi's airport was nice and busy. The air hostess made sure for us to enjoy the visit. When the time was ready for us to go back to the plane, we found out that the plane had a malfunction and we will not leave the same day. The airlines arranged for us to stay in the airport hotel for the night with two airhostesses. I heard the pilot ordering for our families to be notified about the delay, that we are safe and we will be taken care of.

The next morning the hostess awakened us to get ready to go to the airport to catch our plane heading to Basra, Iraq.

Dara Ship

The daughter and son of the Patel family to the left and me to the right

Famous Bhilar Table Land

My Iraqi and Bangkok friends and I

The Krishna Valley (River)

Me, in School wearing the traditional Indian outfit (Sari)

The St. Joseph Boarding School Students in Panchgani-India

St. Joseph School in Panchgani drill Performance.

Sixteenth Birthday   With my Godson   My Indian roommate
with my friend

Chapetr 16

When you finally go back to your old hometown,
you find it wasn't the old home you missed but your
childhood
-."Sam Ewing

Coming back home from India

I returned back home with another Iraqi student from Basra. We took the Plane from Bombay to Basra with one stop in Karachi (Pakistan).

The airlines did send a telegram to our families informing them that we will arrive the next day. Two airhostesses accompanied us to a hotel by the airport and stayed with us, since we were underage. I was scared and wondering what is going to happen to us. In these countries no one can give us guarantees to be safe. I was worried about myself and I learned in strange situations that I needed to pray.

We spent the night at the hotel and the next morning the airhostesses ordered breakfast for us before we headed to the airport to catch our plane to Basra. We were scared and praying to get home safe.

As the plane took off, we were more relaxed and we were looking forward to see our families. The time I spent in Bombay I had friends who taught me how to use face makeup. I liked it and I thought I was old enough to put on lipstick. That was what I did before the plane landed at Basra International Airport. I put on some make-up thinking that I was ready to see my family.

As the plane landed and the passengers started leaving the plane going down the stairs we did the same. We started looking for our families and sure enough, I found my parent, sisters, brothers, aunts, uncles and my grandfather standing behind the fence waiving to us. As we walked down from the plane to the check- point room to show our passports and clear our luggage, I let the other student go ahead of me. Then I completed my papers and was grabbing my luggage.

To my surprise, two of my aunts grabbed my arms, one from each, side, and ran with me to the ladies room to the sink to wash my face before my grandfather saw me.

I did not resist them because I learned to respect the elderly. I said to them that I did not do anything wrong. They said the make-up is wrong and they do not use makeup in my grandfather's presence.

Later on, they explained to me that I was too young to use make-up and my grandfather will never allow it, even for them, since they were not married. I accepted the situation knowing how my culture is and I respect it.

I was happy to be home. However, when I returned home, I found out that most of my close friends were scattered all around the country. Most of my friends I was not able to connect with. Some of the Jewish friends had left the country and others relocated or left Basra to attend other schools.

Our home was full of action and busy with visitors coming to see me after a long time being away from the country. When I left to India there was no TV service in Basra. Coming back, to my surprise, my parents had TV but it was broadcasting from Iran and speaking Farsi, which we were not able to understand. We watched Indian and Persian movies without understanding the languages. At first you would enjoy it, but it became boring. There was not much to do.

After a few weeks my cousin (my mother's sister son) came from Baghdad. I was happy to see him and we needed to catch up. Then I found out that his father sent him to take me back to Baghdad. I was surprised that my parents were not opposed to the idea.

Memories took me back to me when I spent all the weekends and holidays with my cousins since my aunt and uncle loved having me, and considered me as their daughter. I was one year older than him and his parents always thought of me as their older daughter. Meanwhile, we made the best of the time while he was with us. After few days later, I packed again and we were on our way to Baghdad. We took the train. It was a good trip I always loved riding the train. The noise of the train is very soothing and relaxing.

As the train was moving and I had my head on the backrest, memories started coming back about how I was wanted by my cousins and they loved me as their older sister, although we were close in age. Growing up between two homes, as in America it was similar to "Joined Custody". That's how I felt living with my parents during the school days and living with my aunt and uncle during the weekends and holidays.

We talked all the way. I updated him about my trip to India and he was surprised that I was mixing English with Arabic words when speaking. I explained to him the situation in school "what do you expect when I was in school 24/7 and everyone is speaking English? I found out as he told me later on that he also spoke English with the American Jesuits School in Baghdad where he is attending at the time. We were occupied sharing our experiences, time was going fast and we fell asleep.

We woke up in the morning it was 8:00 am and found ourselves with train approaching Baghdad's station. Around 9:00 am the train stated approaching Baghdad Station. We were looking from the window for his parents and we saw them and talked to them through the open window. At the station my uncle and aunt were there to pick us up without my other cousins. I asked about the rest of the cousins and I was informed that they are in school. My cousins are three sons and two daughters, and basically I grew up with them as part of their family.

Baghdad looked different to me. It seemed more crowded than before. We arrived at the house and my uncle could not believe that I was there. He instructed his son to take me with his sisters to the movies that night. So my cousin picked a nice movie for us to go and see with his two sisters, since his other two younger brothers boys were to stay home. Shortly, my other cousins came from school and it felt great to be with them again. I felt love around me we grew up together all our life. I was one year older than my cousin and he was the oldest of all his siblings.

We made several calls to Basra, to my parents to tell them that we arrived safely. (When I think about the situation how my parents sent me with no question to leave home when I had just arrived from India).

I believe that my parents as well as myself knew how much my aunt, uncle and the cousins loved me.

We spent most of the day talking about my stay in India. My aunt and uncle and their children were curious how it was for me living with a strange culture. I told them that I was used to being away from my parents. I made friends with other girls and enjoyed their company. My cousins (the girls) were interested in details and how our daily schedule was. I told my cousins about the daily routine such going to church every morning and our outing for a walk where sometimes we see the boys from St. Mary's going on their own routine walk. We were taught not to look at them or smile.

I found out my cousins were interested when I started talking about the Monsoon rainy season and how the rain was unusual, not like what we had in the winter. Describing how the rain used to be pouring with thunder continuously for days and sometimes for weeks. Finally I informed them about the mango trees, heavily loaded with fruits. Some would fall on the ground and we would pick some to take back to the school. To eat them by pealing the mango that are not ripe and the inside was white. We sliced them and sprinkle salt and red pepper; yam yam they were delicious.

My cousins tried to accommodate me to feel comfortable showing me the house and the bedrooms. They helped taking my suite case to the bedrooms. We kept on talking trying to catch up with what we missed for those years.

Later that day we were getting ready to go to the movies. I was busy talking to my cousin about his driving the car and he said that there was no age limit and his dad trusted him driving. We were excited and ready to go out to the movies I felt I am back and I am the favorite one in the house as it was before. However, the girls did not show anything in front of their father and mother since they knew surely that I was the mostly favored by their father just like the boys and the mother always agreed.

My uncle and my aunt in Baghdad ignored my parent's constantly calling and demanding that I should be going back home and they challenged them and they kept me. As a matter of fact my uncle registered me at the American Institute to learn business and office Administration focusing on Typing and shorthand. He was taking me back and forth to the Institute. That course took me 6 months to complete. He was proud of me, that I finished with honors.

During weekdays, when my cousins were doing homework for school, my aunt and uncle took me out with them out when they visited their relatives and friends. I was introduced as part of the family as I grew up with the children and was considered the older sister. I started enjoying the preference, knowing that was the situation since we were children.

One time my aunt and I went to visit friends for the first time after my return from India. This family had been a distant relative from my grandmother's side. The daughters loved me and I enjoyed being with them. While we were, there two of their neighbors sent messages that they are interested to come to their home and get introduced. to me. That was a proposal to ask for my hand. The Lady of the house turned them off, telling them that I was not ready. This lady of the house (the mother) kept on reminding me of these incidents whenever we see each other.

Time was going so fast and we were enjoying ourselves. My cousin had to juggle between school/homework and spending time with us girls; his sisters and I going out to movies and parties; most going out together was in weekends. He mentioned on time to me that he was distracted and was surprised that he completed his high school with good grades.

Childhood is a promise that is never kept. ~Ken Hill

My stay in Baghdad lasted for 8 months, until my mother and aunts came for a visit and insisted to take me back with her to Basra. I do not know what has been planned between my mom and my uncle about my cousin and me. I could sense that my uncle is serious and wants this to happen but my mother for one reason or another was trying to pull out.

Chapter 17

Back to Basra from Baghdad

My mother made sure that she would not return to Basra without me. I wanted to go back home although my uncle, aunt and the children were not happy for me to leave. My uncle and his son tried to convince me to stay, but I had to follow my mother's guidance.

Basra seemed different and I started asking lots of questions. I realized that the country has gone through peaceful changes of political regime. My family never participated in politics so it was nothing for me to worry about. However, the change for me was I lost contact with my friends. For me things appeared not the same and I felt lonely, although my family life before was involved in the church social activities.

My older sister was working and my younger sister was going to school and of course my younger brothers were in school too. I wanted to work but my parents thought that I was too young to work at age 18. Finally. I had an option of two jobs one in a bank and the other was with an insurance Company. My parents agreed, to go to school first and then work. But I managed to convince them that I would do both.

Therefore, I started working in a bank with international accounts. I was working mainly with companies who import goods from all over the world. I was the only Iraqi employee qualified with English and French languages and office management. I was working directly with the bank manager (since he did not speak any language other than Arabic). I was making direct contacts internationally.

I was happy working and going to school. In the meantime, I had several marriage offers but I was not ready. My uncle from Baghdad made an unexpected visit to Basra. He stated that he had to attend a very important meeting. He talked to me about my job and how I like working at the bank. I told him that I feel good and no one bothers me. He said to me, "you know I feel that you are the same as my own daughters and I have to check on you". He brought me two appointment books, one for work and the other for my own journal. He presented them as from my cousins.

My uncle left for Baghdad feeling relieved knowing that he needs to keep checking on me and keep being involved in my life. He considered me like his oldest daughter and I could tell he was afraid that he would lose me as a daughter. I was in contact with my cousin's family and I was busy working at the bank. It was a good job and I enjoyed the attention from the foreign and local customers, co-workers and the special recognition from admiration.

My job was to prepare the document for the import and export planning and trading for the International Merchants making arrangements for shipping corps. I enjoyed my job and learned a lot about trading and bartering in the goods industry. I learned when the ships were in or out and the merchandise that was traded.

I kept myself busy between working at the bank and going to school. During this period I visited Baghdad with my mother and we stayed with her sister. My uncle, cousin and the family were happy to see me back. We had a good visit for only one week because I needed to go back to work and school.

Returning to Basra was great; I loved Basra especially in the evenings. I enjoyed the evening walk along the riverfront of Shatt Al-Arab, having a pleasurable experience with the Arabian Jasmine's delicate fragrance, along the municipal homes fence.

Out of the blue, my uncle, my mother's brother, approached me to work as his executive secretary for his company. I requested a few days to think about the offer and he agreed saying, "take your time". As usual, whenever I am about to make a major decision usually, I pray to God for guidance. I prayed for God to give me a sign. After few days later, I talked to my uncle that I am ready to take the job.

I had things to take care of including outstanding paperwork and submitting my resignation. It took me several days and management was OK with that, since my uncle is a good customer of the bank. The following week, I started working with my uncle. I enjoyed working and the attention was on me, since I was the only girl there. All the employees' gave me a special attention.

My uncle and I were a team. We worked together and travelled together. I was his favorite niece. Our relationship became closer. He was proud of me, and he used to introduce me to his customers and friends that visited him as his favorite niece that had her education in India.

I started working and it was different from the bank atmosphere. I was the only girl in the office. I kept myself busy arranging the paperwork and writing business letters. The training that I had in Baghdad came in handy. I continued to attend school in the evening.

After a few months, I found my older sister coming to the office for a visit. I was surprised; I asked her why she came. She said to me that she heard that there was someone who came from Baghdad and he saw me at work and he had asked for my hand in marriage. I did not notice anything, even though I knew that someone arrived from Baghdad from the main office to check on the agency; meaning my uncle. It appeared to me that my sister wanted to see the guy. In the Chaldean/Iraqi culture, it was not favored that the younger sister gets married before the older sister.

After work I went home and I asked my mother why she did not tell me and I had to hear it from my older sister. My mom apologized that she heard about it the same day I heard. However, my sister heard from a colleague at work. Then my mother said that" this young man saw you and he wants to come and visit us." My answer to my mom was that I would take my time and my dad thought, that I was young to get married. I was confused myself, but my mother assured me that no one will rush me and I need to take my time to make the decision.

The following day my mother called me to inform me that we are going to have a visitor coming to talk to us. My uncle was in Europe at that time for a business trip. Since the person who proposed to me has worked with the company for many years, and my uncle knew him personally, my parents sent my uncle a telegram informing him about the proposal. My uncle's response was "I have no problem in approving this man who is a good individual and has good education and steady job. Salma has my blessing, but the final decision should be hers".

Our visitor came that day for tea. He had a friend and distant relative who resided in Basra and know my family. It is customary to accept a proposal that is made by a person with someone who knows the family to be reliable and trustworthy. The visit was just to let my parent know that he is interested and has good intentions in my hand in marriage and for me to be able to see him. We would be able to talk on the phone after our approval. This is the process in the Chaldean culture in order to be engaged at that time.

After they left, my parents said that I have to make up my mind. Everyone liked him and had positive feedback about him. My extended family received the message and my mother started making phone calls to the priest asking about his family name. The priest gave a very high recommendation that the proposed individual comes from a very good family.

His mother on the other hand called her cousin when she learned that my aunt lives on the same street as her cousin. His mother's cousin informed his mother "If this is the same girl I am thinking of that spent 6-8 months in Baghdad, I know for sure that she, was the same girl who spent the spring and summer with her aunt and uncle." His family was confused and wanted an answer. My future to be fiancé called my aunt in Baghdad and asked her if he can visit them.

At that time, I was not informed what the intention of the visit was. About a few weeks later, my uncle from Baghdad made a surprised visit to Basra. Being my uncle's favorite and respected niece I was always straight and direct with him as he is with me. So I asked him what was exactly the nature of his visit? And his answer to me was that my future fiancé wants an answer from me. I said to him, "I am still thinking".

I thought that it was strange for my uncle to make a trip to Basra just to talk to me and find out that I was free to make my own decision. I did not make my decision every time he opened the subject. Then on his last day he said to me that he will be leaving the next day and he hope to get a final answer from me.

One of the important things I learned from the French nuns is to pray before making an important decision, especially a lifetime commitment. Praying is important for me when it comes to decision making which always helped me in the long-term. I kept on praying for God's guidance to direct and lead me to make the final decision.

As my uncle's time to leave became close, I knew that he would want my final and ultimate decision. We all took him to the airport. He finally took me aside and asked me for the last time if I made my decision. I remember saying to him "yes I accept the proposal". I said it as if someone else was saying it with me. I looked at my uncle and I remember that there was a big disappointment on his face with my decision, but he never questioned me then or after that.

Chapter 18

Getting engaged to be married

In this chapter my focus comes together on my true story of faith, commitment and courage to succeed in life. Part of my culture during my childhood I was always guided by my parents and my extended family. However, later as I was growing up I found myself taking responsibility of my own decisions. I became conscious toward my surroundings and aware of my own thoughts and needs.

As I was growing older I started feeling different as if something is changing within me. I experienced an overwhelming change. A flow of moving sudden movement began happening I started noticing power that influenced every aspect of my life. I began making my own decisions that created for me a very strong personality. I grew up with faith and confidence that were imbedded in my mind. I was and still am a great believer with faith and prayer in asking God for guidance.

> *Doubt sees obstacles*
> *Faith sees the way*
> *Doubt sees the darkest night*
> *Faith sees the day.*
> ~ Author Unknown~

Another aspect was my leaving my country to go to India; that had a huge impact on changing the way I looked at my life. I realized by now that I have been changed. The change was that being in the boarding school I was able to pray for any move I made. I found out that I had God's guidance in every step in my life.

Marriages in the Chaldean culture usually arranged by two families, for compatibility (education, family status, religion and age). Both families come to an agreement and then the decision is left to the couple to decide.

My American friends always said to that love come before the marriage. However the Iraqi Chaldeans believe that love comes after the wedding and the marriage last.

We also, believe that marriage is more likely to survive when the culture emphasize a significant attachment as we heard all the time "remember there is no divorce." We knew that if we get married we have to love the person and make the marriage work for life. This influences the couple to adjust and make compromises. We believe that love grows with the relationship and the couple meets half way in making their life decisions.

My father did not like the idea of my marriage; he thought I was still too young. So, the decision was mine to make. It was a tremendous struggle for me. On the other hand, I wanted to fall in love, and then get married yet I knew this was not the accepted in Iraq. I also did not want to be the first in my family to get married. My older sister was not married and, in Iraqi culture, typically the older daughter marries first. Some parents refuse to let the younger daughter to marry first and try to push the older one.

After a full month of radical negotiating with my family in Basra and my extended family in Baghdad, I made my decision to get married. It was hard for me, since I was the first one in my family and among my cousins to get married. I was (19) too young to leave my family to live with my husband.

My fiancé came to visit my family and I few times (since he lived in Baghdad). He used to call most of the time and we talked on the phone. He made special visits for our traditional and official engagement. The priest would come to the home to bless the couple and pray for a blessed engagement time together; he also blessed the rings. My parents invited all the extended family and some close friends. My fiancé brought with him from Baghdad his mother and his older sister.

There was a band that played the music and a singer, as we danced together for the first time with the family blessing. Champagne was served to the guest and us for a toast. Dinner and desert were served.

There is not much tradition to Iraqi Christians that does not match any American wedding. Iraqi Christian is referred to in Iraq as the modern folks. I am saying this since I am Iraqi Christian/Chaldean and my husband had the same background.

The weddings I attended use either Arabic food catering or just depend on a nice dinner "steak, chicken or fish." Most of the parties are hosted in banquet Room, country clubs or private Banquet Rooms and you just have to choose the food that the hall offers.

The Chaldeans speak the Aramaic language which is the language spoken by Jesus Christ. Chaldeans hold a henna party, either a few days or the night before the wedding. It is custom to give the bride lots of gold. There is also tradition of inviting the older ladies to view the bedroom and set up the bed with new sheets, and towels, anything that is new that is going to be used for the future home.

During the wedding day, both homes of the bride and groom are busy with close family from each side and close friends. A prepared table full with sweets and snacks is served before the church ceremony. The bride and the groom to leave the home with music and the family dancing escorting them separately each one from their own home to the limo to take them to church. The groom is dressed with his tuxedo. Traditionally, he will wear a ribbon on the side of arm with few crosses on it for blessings and good luck.

It is important that all the ceremony and tradition is done with one thing in mind: marrying at a Catholic Church means divorce or separation is not accepted. Also divorced couple cannot re-marry someone else since the church will not accept their marriage. So the marriage is sacred and the couple takes this very seriously.

After the church, the bride and groom take their time to take pictures with the wedding party and freshen up to attend the celebration of their wedding party. The precision starts for the bride and groom, which is done by announcing the names of the wedding party, starting with the flower girl, ring boy, the bride maids and the groomsmen's couples, and finally the groom and bride. They will enter on a traditional "Khiga" line dance with music and lots of colored scarves that have coins attached to their end. This might take up to 45 minutes. The grooms' family might also during the party give the bride some gold and they will be showing it to people by dressing her up. There are traditional line dances "Debkah" and belly dancer. This is a customary wedding.

My wedding

My wedding was planned to be in Baghdad at the home church of the groom, my husband to be. My parents, brothers and sisters and I travelled by train to Baghdad. The train had sleeping compartments. Few of my aunts and uncles accompanied us on the train. Others drove to Baghdad. Driving took about 6 hours and by train 12 hours. I had too much luggage only the wedding gown had a large traveling bag. Traveling at night was great. Each compartment holds four passengers; two up and two down. It was fun.

Although those were the last few days to spend with my family as single girl, I was overwhelmed and did not think about what was going on around me. I was content and just enjoying the time as it came.

My mother and the aunts brought nuts, sandwiches, vegetables, fruits and cookies that we ate while watching the canary from the window. The train conductor was helpful and gave us great service, especially when he found out that there was a bride to be on his shift. The conductor visited once more before we finally lay in our beds with warm covers to sleep.

The sound of the train put us to sleep quicker. We woke up when the train made a stop by a small city called Artawi, which is by the Marshes where water buffalo are raised and women sell the dairy product to the train passengers. They make the best buffalo clotted cream. My parents bought some to eat for breakfast with fresh bread baked the same day. That used to be the best treat riding the train.

After breakfast we washed and changed to be ready when the train reached the Baghdad train station. Very soon we were by the windows approaching the city I can see my aunt, uncle, my fiancé and his sisters standing on the side to welcome us and be hospitable.

As we gathered our luggage to get them off the train, we greeted everyone and we were headed to my uncle's home to stay in their house until my wedding day. The children were in school. I was the first one to get married from my family and the cousins.

My fiancé wanted me to ride in his car with my parents and we headed to my uncle's home. Half way, he then said that his mother wanted us to stop over their home to see me before we go to my uncle's home.

We stopped at my future home. It looked different from my parent's home. I had no doubt that I will be happily married with my future husband. It was like a dream, the days were passing so fast from the day we arrived to Baghdad to the wedding day.

We spent one week in Baghdad before our wedding. We were invited to my fiancée's immediate family homes to be introduced to the whole family.

Time went so fast I could not slow it. I knew I was making the right decision since I had my God and my faith that things will work well for me. I tried to take time off to be with myself to be able to make the connection with God, hoping that I was doing the right thing but things were going too fast for me. With my faith and God's guidance, I knew deep inside that God would be with me all the way.

Our wedding was different since we arranged to take the plane for our honeymoon directly after the church's ceremony. We left the same day for the honeymoon. The wedding day was the third day of Easter (Tuesday). The plane was scheduled to leave Baghdad to Beirut, Lebanon on Tuesday and Thursday only. All the wedding arrangements' were planned around the departure time for our honeymoon.

As I entered the church with my uncle, since he was like the Godfather of the family, I never asked my mom why he had to walk me down the isle. My mother was a very strong lady and my father always catered to her needs. As we were walking down the aisle, my fiancé met us half way and together we walked down the Alter. During this time, I was busy praying faithfully asking, God's guidance to do the right thing.

My fiancé arranged a large seven-layer cake to be served with champagne in a very elegant setting outside the church with waiters to serve the guests after the wedding ceremony. The family and guests enjoyed the two-hour celebration cutting the cake and making a toast with cake and champagne. We took too many pictures with our friends and relatives.

Time went so fast. Before we know it, we had to leave the reception and thanked the guests for being with us on our wedding day. After we said our goodbye to the guests we left the church to the house to change out of our wedding outfits taking our luggage on our way to the Baghdad International Airport.

My family and the in-laws were there at the airport waiting for us. We socialized with the family and some close friends who came to say their goodbyes to us. My in-laws were happy that we are leaving to enjoy the honeymoon. On the other hand my family as usual were crying and at the same time were happy that we were going to spend some time with my grandfather in Beirut.

The flight was two hours to Beirut International Airport. When the plane was ready to land it was amazing to see the scenery looking down on the city of Beirut, surrounded by the mountains. I was tired and sleepy and wanted badly to catch my bed. My eyes were closing and I was fighting it to stay awake. After the plane landed, we walked through customs and the workers at the airport know we were newly married couple since many newly wed couples spent their honeymoon in Lebanon. As we walked through the airport, were greeted by the airport employees wishing us good luck.

We took a taxicab to the hotel that was facing the Mediterranean Sea. It was a breath- taking scene when we stood on the balcony watching the sea and the sound of the waves breaking the silence of the night. My husband ordered some sandwiches and fruits and we talked as we were eating.

It was a beautiful view. However, I was tired and was ready to sleep. Our plan was to sleep and the next morning we will relax and have breakfast on the balcony facing the Mediterranean Sea. We talked as we changed, getting ready to sleep since we were exhausted and worn-out. Without realizing the time, I fell asleep.

The next morning we woke up and took a shower and changed to be ready to start our day. We ordered breakfast and before our order came we received a phone call from the hotel's front desk saying there was a visitor asking for us. My husband asked to talk to the visitor. It was my grandfather who lived in Lebanon came to greet us. My husband invited him to the room to have breakfast with us.

Little did we know how significantly our honeymoon was interrupted!

Chapter 19

Honeymoon: From Baghdad to Lebanon

My grandfather was happy to see me. I was his first granddaughter to get married. We enjoyed our first breakfast together and I was happy to be with my grandfather.

After we were done with breakfast, my grandfather broke the news to us by saying to us, "pack-you two are coming to my house on the mountain to stay with me for the entire honeymoon." I looked at my husband puzzled, how we are going to enjoy our honeymoon? My husband was very polite and he accepted the offer and we packed and left the hotel riding my grandfather's car.

As we were riding the car, he was asking about the family and how the wedding was asked who attended the wedding. He started telling us he knew we were going to Beirut for our honeymoon and he wanted to be there with us. In no time we were on the top of the mountain. The view was beautiful and spectacular with the valley down on the Cedar trees, shooting high, covered with the pine nuts.

My Grand father

Now, I am thinking my grandfather from my mother's side. He was well known in Basra, social and involved with the Chaldean Church. As an Armenian genocide survivor, my grandfather like my dad, they were quite to themselves.

My father was gentle and quiet. My grandfather on the other hand, was the same, but as I heard from my aunt he was uptight when it came to his own children, especially the boys.

I believe that his traumatic childhood made him hard on his own children and was not able to show them the love that we grand children experienced. I am saying this because I did not know his background until I was married and left to Lebanon for our honeymoon with my husband.

At that time my, grand father was retired from his job in Basra and decided to visit Lebanon. Lebanon is known as the Switzerland of the Middle East. (As I mentioned in the past chapters.)

My grand father invited us to stay in his resort on the mountain that he built for his retirement with the children and grand children when we visited Lebanon.

We were not able to say no to him so we went along to stay with him and my aunt (my mother's sister), she chose to stay single since her mother died devoting her life for her father, her siblings and their children. She acted like her own mother would be if she was alive. My aunt was very happy to see me since I was the first niece to get married, and as a bride to stay with them on my honeymoon with my husband.

The house was large and three story levels and each level has it's own kitchen and bath and bedrooms for privacy. The house was seated on the top of the mountain over looking the valley and the town Falougha.

My grandfather was known by the local Lebanese as the Iraqi who lives in the big house on the mountain. In the center of the town there was a roundabout with a garden in the middle and some benches for people to sit and enjoy the cool weather.

My grandfather was very happy for me, his first grad-daughter to be married, and wanted the whole town to see my husband and me. His friends in that town respected him and people were pleased to see him cheerful welcoming us as the newly wed couple. His friends and neighbors welcomed us to their homes.

We spent the time visiting, shopping and going on the beach in the daytime and at night we spent the time going to nightclubs. There were several families who were close friends with my grandfather's family who invited us to their home whenever we had free time in between our activities. As for transportation and outings we, were taken care of by a family who were close to my grandfather.

We were always well taken care by friends who offered their services to take us everywhere day or night. We were very comfortable with one of the family members that my husband became close to, Faris, who became our guide and took us everywhere. We became very close to him and later on, our first son we named him Faris.

As usual one day Faris took my aunt and myself shopping at downtown Beirut and sight seeing. We had chicken where it was their specialty (Rotisserie chicken). After we were done, Faris changed the route to show me the waterfall that comes from a spring with the best water you can drink that supplies all the drinking water in Lebanon. This spring was close to my grandfather's home (about three miles and a half).

On our way back about half way we were stopped by a checkpoint monitored by the Syrian troops. They asked for our identifications. My aunt and Faris had theirs but I did not have my passport with me since my husband kept all our documents including my passport. The soldier asked me to step out of the car and insisted that he needs to see some identification or they need to go home and bring my identification in order to be released. So we were told that they would keep me with them until someone will bring my passport.

Faris and my aunt tried to reason with the soldiers that I was on my honeymoon and to let me go, but they did not care. My aunt was smart and she told Faris that she will stay with me and for him she instructed him to go to the house and bring my passport from my husband.

I gave a hug to my aunt whispering to her that I was scared and prayed that God to be with me to keep me safe from these soldiers. I was glad that my aunt stayed with me. We sat outside the tent praying for my husband and Faris to come quick. That, one hour seemed like four hours of waiting. Finally, my husband and Faris came with my passport and I was released. We immediately headed home.

The story was all over town that; "the Iraqi bride was held by the Syrian troops for not having a passport on her". We started hearing stories about young women disappearing in incidents similar to my situation. For a longtime my husband would hug me and we thanked God that we are safe to go back home.

The two- week stay in Lebanon went so fast and we returned home to Baghdad. It was hard to say good-bye to my grandfather, my aunts and the families we met in Lebanon. For a while, I had nightmares about that incident.

Arriving in Baghdad, as a newly wed couple the Chaldean tradition is that close family and friends visit us to congratulate us, and welcome me to the family. Friends and family members also invited us to their homes since it is expected traditionally.

We visited Lebanon another time after my first son was born and we named him Faris. We did not stay with my grandfather. We rented a home in Falougha for three months and my husband wanted to have his privacy and we were expecting some of his family to visit and they can stay with us.

It was great. That was the last time I saw my grandfather. After we immigrated to the States we received the news that he was killed in his home in Falougha. Lebanon was going through a civil war and no one was able to uncover his killers. It was a tragic incident for our family and every time we visit Lebanon, we visit his home that is boarded. My tears come down remembering the happy time we spent there.

My grandfather

My husband and I in our honeymoon

Chapter 20

"God gave us memory so that we might have roses in December."
~"http://www.goodreads.com/author/show/5255014.
J_M_Barrie" **J.M. Barrie**~

Living in Baghdad with my husband

I moved to Baghdad (the Capital of Iraq) where my husband lived with his family. Baghdad was totally different from Basra, socially limited and spacious. Since Basra is a smaller city with two Chaldean churches, community members were known either by family name or by first name. On the other hand, Baghdad was large and I felt lost. However, my husband and his family were well known to the Christian community and they were considerate of my situation and did what they could to make things easier for me.

My husband had a large extended family. From my side, I had only my aunt Alice, my uncle and their children, who were waiting for me to come back. I lived with them during the holidays back in Basra before they moved to Baghdad.

Since my husband was the youngest of his siblings, his oldest sister was married and had a daughter before he was born. That is why my husband was close to his nieces and nephews, being almost the same age.

My husband's nieces and nephews were waiting for me since I was younger than they were and they knew that we were going to get along fine. Everyone in my husband's family treated me like a princess. I spent most of my time with them when my husband was on business trips.

We were very happily married. I believe I came to love my husband by his constant love, respect and tenderness toward me. Since he travelled on the job outside Baghdad, he made arrangements with his sister, who had daughters my age and older, to pick me up, to spend time with when he was gone on a business trip.

A few months later, my husband surprised me by hiring a driver (George) to take me around when he was not in town since his car was in the garage. One day when my husband was out of town, I asked George to teach me how to drive. My husband's car was a German car with a stick shift engine. George had no problem and he took me to an empty parking lot and started with the basics, such as how to shift the gears.

George was a true gentleman and very respectful toward me. I felt safe when I was with him. After four driving lessons I started driving to my aunt's house. Everyone was thrilled to see me driving on my own. Later, the same day I visited my husband's sister. Everyone felt intense excitement to see me driving alone, which meant I will be able to visit them more often.

After a few days I called George to take me shopping. I surprised him with the news that I drove alone to my aunt's house. He was thrilled and he said to me "you probably don't need me any more." I said to him "George I will never be able to drive to downtown Baghdad in the crowded streets. Anyway my husband doesn't know about my driving yet". I felt that had steadily gained my confidence and freedom. I had no driver's license, but that did not stop me from driving. I enjoyed my independence. My husband encouraged me to drive on the main roads and he said I needed a valid driver's license.

The next step was to call my uncle in Basra who has friends in the police department to get me a drive's license. Soon I received my driver's license in the mail without a test. This is a country that confirm the saying, "Its not what you know; Its whom you know" Anyway, I was thrilled with the driver's license.

However, my mother-in-law did not like it; she thought I was given too much freedom. My husband instructed me to do the right thing and he will support me and not allow anyone to ever be able to say anything to me. I then became pregnant soon after we married, and I wanted to enjoy my self-independence before the baby to be born.

We were traveling all over Iraq. My husband amazed me with his accurate assessment to the roads, from one city to another with an accurate time we will reach the next point. We also visited Basra, my hometown more often and my family was happy to see us. Whenever we visited Basra my mom would invite special friends and relatives to see my husband and me.

Most of our friends remembered me as a child, and now I am married and pregnant, expecting my first son. At that moment reality hit me I missed Basra and I missed being a child at my parent's home. I was everyone's favorite and used to feel it most of the time when friends and family made comments about the way I dressed up and the way I handled myself.

Cultural shock

The first summer in Baghdad, it was very hot since the weather in Baghdad is dry and hot in summer. My husband came back from work and after we had our lunch, we decided to take a nap. This is usual to all the Iraqis since the day is long and a siesta is a must during the hot summer months. This was the norm all over Iraq, since all jobs worked from 8:30 am to 2:00 pm. Vacation time was a month to two months a year, not counting the Muslim's Holidays and the Christian's Holidays.

One day in the afternoon while we were sleeping in Baghdad, my mother in-law knocked at our bedroom door saying that the lady next door is coming for tea to congratulate us on our marriage and meet the bride.

Without delay, I woke up my husband and passed on the message that his mother conveyed to me. We started dressing up getting ready to meet the neighbor. I asked my husband who is this neighbor? He seemed not to know her, and yet his mother had good relationships with the neighbors. He said to me, this is good for you to spend your mornings visiting the neighbors.

We walked down the stairs on our way to the living room with me leading. As I entered the room with a big smile, I greeted the lady with my husband behind me. I was shocked to see the lady trying to cover her face and chest, not wanting to be seen as she was. My husband was so scared that he left the room immediately.

She instantly turned to my mother-in-law politely telling her, "How could you bring a man to the room and I am not covered?" My mother-in-law was speechless and did not know how to deal with the situation. We kept on telling her that we made a mistake and did not mean it. I tried talk to her and let her know that this was an innocent mistake, but she insisted on leaving the house.

We all were shocked, tried to calm the woman, but she was upset, saying that no man has seen her without the Abaya to cover herself and she left right away to her home. I never saw her again. That was the first time to experience such an attitude that I was not accustomed to. Even in Basra, we had friends who are Muslims who never acted that way. She caught us off guard.

In spite what happened, I believe it was an isolated incident. And at that time, I had never had a similar experience in the past with any of our Muslim women in Basra acting that way. All my parent's Muslim friends used to socialize and visit and eat and have fun with our parents, and joke with us husbands and wives. They never covered themselves at that time. That's why growing-up in Basra, we were not able to differentiate between Christians and Muslims.

Today things are different; in Iraq as well as in the Arab world and traditions have been brought to the western world. I remember when I worked in Dearborn, Michigan in the 90's where the city was heavily populated with Muslim refugees after the first attack on Iraq. The Iraqi women were sickened the way they were forced to cover their heads (the Hijab). One lady said to me, "we never wore this in Iraq." My answer to her that this is a free country, you can do what ever you want. Her reply was that people will talk in a bad way about them or behind their backs.

Chapter 21

Moving Back to Basra

My husband was transferred to Basra. I was thrilled to go back to my hometown. I was pregnant with my first baby. My parents, siblings, aunts and uncles were happy and waiting to receive a new addition to the family. I was very comfortable in Basra since I did not like Baghdad. Baghdad had a different culture and the people were not as social as they Basra's happy-go-lucky and easygoing people.

> *"Basra's residents were famous with their social and generous personality."*

My husband was busy with his work, traveling north and south. When he was in Basra, we visited my extended family or went to the Feyha's Club occasionally (this was a private club was for Christians member only). Some members invited Muslim and Jewish families. By this time, my husband was able to make friends with other families and was able to socialize more with my parents' friends and others that we made new friends with.

My husband had to go often to Baghdad. Sometimes he traveled by plane, when he was meeting with the managers in Baghdad. Other times, when he had to visit the agents between Basra and Baghdad, we drove together. Sometimes, we spent a day or two in cities along the way to visit the agents that do business with his Company. I enjoyed those mini trips. Sometimes we stayed few weeks in Baghdad.

We started taking advantage of being free, to enjoy our freedom before the baby was born. We travelled a lot and I started to connect with some of my childhood friends who were left in Basra. I found out that most of them relocated and my Jewish friends had secretly left the country.

I started showing my pregnancy and my friends and relatives were excited to see my stomach getting larger. My mother's aunt (aunty Mary) was picking me up everyday to go for a walk. She said that walking will help me to have an easy delivery. I remember some of the guys who had an eye on me would go back and forth in their cars looking at me being pregnant. I stayed in Basra to have my delivery by our family's mid-wife, who delivered my siblings and I.

My husband was in Basra waiting for the birth of the baby. I was delayed for about three weeks. In the midst of the time of waiting, my husband had a business emergency and he needed to travel to Baghdad on a business trip for couple days.

However, the night my husband left Basra I had the contraction, and I was told that I might have the baby the next day. My mother called the mid-wife to be prepared to come early the next day to check on me.

Sure enough the next day I had my baby at my parent's home without my husband. However the mid-wife was warm, caring and loving which made the delivery easy on me. I had a 10 lb. healthy baby boy.

The first month, my mother kept the baby in her room wanting me to sleep and rest. I was told by my mother and the midwife; that the woman uses all her muscles during the delivery and it takes her 40 days to get back to normal. I was advised to take it easy and not to strain myself.

A week after the delivery the mid wife Ms Farida came to visit me and bathe me the first time after the delivery as a customary thing. My mother prepared the Turkish Bath. The mid-wife as a usual customary gave me a massage as said that usually when a woman deliver a baby using a lot of energy since I just had the baby. I need to take it easy and not exhaust myself. It was great experience, relaxing and soothing and soon I was ready to go to sleep. Friends and relatives were excited to see the progress.

My husband was thrilled. His cultural upbringing had taught him to prefer boys rather than girls, and he was pleased to bring happiness to his mother. We stayed in Basra for a few weeks; according to my mother I needed to rest for forty days after birth of our son.

After two months we had to go back to Baghdad to make arrangements for the baptism of our son at my husband's family church. All my family, aunts and uncles travelled to Baghdad for the baptism. This was the first grand child from my side of the family and everyone wanted to be part of the event.

After the baptism we went back home and my husband's family had prepared dinner. They invited everyone who attended the baptism. We had a good time with my family, cousins, uncles and aunts. Also present were my husband's sisters, with their husbands and children who lived in Baghdad.

It took a few months for reality to sink in, most of the time living with my in-laws while my husband traveled on business trips. At this time, I realized that we were not going to be able to travel with the baby like before. I will be tied up with my son far away from Basra and my family. Thank God I was able to drive and make visits to my aunt's house or to my husband's sister with her daughters who loved me and would take my son to relieve me.

My husband was busy with his job travelling all over the country. Living with my in-laws was hard. My husband's older sisters were not married, living in the same house. With me young being naïve, they wanted to control me. I was smart enough not to allow anyone to control me. I was glad that my husband was open-minded and he did not listen to their complaints that I had too much of freedom. Every time my husband leaves I get more complaints from his mother that I do not stay home.

My husband recommended that I invite his sisters to come with me, since I am going to see relatives. When I did invited them they refused and came with different excuses. I started doing my own things. Thanks to God my husband was transferred to Mosul North of Iraq.

Chapter 22

Going to Mosul

My husband was transferred to Mosul. I was happy to get away from my in-laws. My husband's niece was studying in a medical University. We invited her to stay with us. I was happy to have her with me, since her family who lived in Baghdad was good to me.

Moving from Basra to the north (Mosul) was a huge step for me. I was alienated from my family and friends, and Mussel has it's own culture. Men and women are separated even a husband and wife cannot walk together. I come from a liberal city to a place where if my husband and I want to visit our neighbors I had to sit in a different room with the women, and he will sit with the men and couples were not allowed to go to the movies together. I hated the situation in Mosul thanks to God that I was blessed with great neighbors

Our neighbors were very nice and they loved me since they found out that I had no family or friends in the city. I had my son who was three months and they had a baby the same age. The family was large and the children lived with their parents in the same house. In that huge home lived about 15 to 20 people. They would call me to go to their house and my husband to go to the large hall called (Mudhief). I was young and willing to adapt to other cultures.

When we came home, my husband would tell me what was discussed and the same with me. Soon my husband hired a 14-year-old live-in maid from one of the adjacent villages to help me and keep me company. By then I felt more comfortable.

After few months, we were able to get a nanny for our son. She was 14 years old and very good with our son when I am busy cooking or when I take a nap. She was also keeping me company when my husband travels to the main office in Baghdad.

Mosul itself as a city was beautiful surrounded by mountains and these mountains were busy in the summer where people stay for the pleasant low temperatures. Mosul is culturally depressed and the people were not friendly.

Mosul is about 400 km north of Baghdad and Iraq's second largest city. It is the center for tourist resorts of northern Iraq, and the north's major center for trade, industry and communications. Mosul is situated in the northwestern part of the country, on the west bank of Tigris, and close to the ruined Assyrian city of Nineveh.

Mosul is called The City of Two Springs, because autumn and spring are very much alike the same there. It is also named The Paradise, The Green, and sometimes described as the Pearl of the North. Mosul has been inhabited since Assyrian times.

Long before Islam, a number of Arab tribes had settled in it, and in later times it played a leading role in the Arab wars of conquest and became a city of great importance. It was an important trade center because of its strategic position on the caravan route between India, Persia and the Mediterranean.

Mosul's chief export was cotton, and today's definition of muslin is derived from the name of the city. Mosel is rich in old historical and ancient buildings; mosques, castles churches, and monasteries, which mostly feature architecturally significant, decorative work.

St Thomas Church is one of the oldest historical church, and named after St. Thomas the Apostle, who preached the Gospel in the East, including in India.

Manna from Heaven

In Iraq, the lines between fact and fiction, history and religion, myth and reality comes this manna from heaven can become irritatingly unclear. That's why some people find it hard to believe when I say that I was lucky to say that I ate the manna from heaven. It's true.

As I stated earlier, when my husband and I lived in Mousel and he traveled all over Iraq, he came back from his trip to Sulemaniah, in

Northern Iraq. He said that the company's agent gave him a large box of manna. I looked at it looked greenish and I thought to myself this is nasty.

My husband explained to me that this is the main ingredient of the manna. My husband stated that in special season and there are different varieties from different sources, but the one he brought is formed by sap that escapes from a tree and that's why it was greenish color from the tree.

I could not believe how this color will turn into white. My husband explained things to me stating that he will bring special people who are specialized in the manna process. It turns out there is a rather mysterious food in this part of the world — the best of it comes from Iraq — that goes by the name of Mann Al-Sama, in Arabic meaning Manna from Heaven.

After a few weeks my husband arranged for two women who specialize in processing the manna. They came with a large 170 quarts pot with a stand and they started a fire with lots of wood. The natural manna was put inside the pot and they were stirring the pot.

They began adding the cane sugar (unprocessed sugar), 100 egg whites added slowly, and they were stirring the pot all night. They added rose water and cardamom and the smell was all over. Meanwhile we were preparing the nuts to mix with the manna walnuts, almonds and pistachio to be mixed separately.

The manna that we made and I had the chance to experience was miraculously real. And it was perfectly delicious.

Now I am talking about it seems parallels between the Quran and the Bible, and Passover and the story of Exodus, a version of which, incidentally, also appears in the Quran.

I am not an expert in recounting the biblical story of the Israelites led by Moses crossing the Sinai desert out of Egypt. We noted that Moses made it all the way to Mount Nebo, just outside Amman, from where he could see the Promised Land he never reached.

During the 40 years in the wilderness, I can relate since I grew up in a Catholic school with Catholic parents where the Bible was frequently discussed. While passing the desert from Egypt the Israelites were hungry and were sent from heaven a strange, wonderful and mysterious food "to be sent from heaven" by God. It turns out the stuff does, in fact, appear out of nowhere — as if from heaven.

It is not a fruit. It is not a baker's or a candy-maker's confection. Instead, it blows in the wind and lands on the ground, generously served by nature, although my nicely packaged gift showed some unmistakably human intervention. Manna may have been a sticky and sweet substance from a plant.

Manna from Heaven

Chapter 23

Returning back to Baghdad

After we had our first son, and moved to Mosul, there were many changes in the business sectors. Private owned companies that were managed by British and Americans were nationalized and my husband's company was one of them. My husband was not comfortable with the change. It was not a good change. Things were changing from bad to worse. New Iraqi managers took over without experience in the field a political affiliation allowed some people to get into the upper level in the company.

My husband never was involved in any political parties. It always could work against you if you are with the wrong party. There was no freedom to choose any party, and if you are with the non-ruling party, you can be jailed or killed. That's why most Christians kept away from politics.

When I was close to having my second baby, I left Mosul to be in Baghdad to be with family and relatives, for the childbirth. Returning to Baghdad was where I had my second son in a private hospital in Baghdad. I had a second boy and natural birth without complications.

By then, I had two boys (11) months difference one right after the other. I became busy with the two children. Thanks to God that the nanny was with me to be taking care of the older son. My mother-in-law was not happy to have her around, even though she used her to clean the house and wash the dishes in her spare time.

I was too busy to think of my stress and my inner needs. I was young myself and did not know how to enjoy my children. Very shortly after my second child was born, I needed a change in my life. So my husband suggested that we could spend the summer in Lebanon. He immediately started making the arrangements for his vacation. One good thing in Iraq is employees can take up-to 4 months vacations (adding sick leave). It was approved right away.

We planned to visit Lebanon again

I was also busy calling my mother to send the 3 months old baby (Mahir) and his nanny to stay with them. My mother was ok with the arrangements. My parents were happy to take care of my baby, since I was the only married daughter and to take care of my son was an honor. I was lucky that my cousin who lived in Baghdad was getting married in Basra and her parents were taking the whole family to Basra for the wedding. They agreed to take with them my baby and his nanny to Basra for my mother to take care of Mahir while we are away.

We knew that we will not be able to handle two infants, so we decided to send the new born with the nanny to Basra to stay with my mother and she will take care of the baby. I trusted my mother since she was great with children and had raised us five children and her nephews and nieces.

Leaving to Lebanon

In June 1966, we left Baghdad and the weather started to warm up in there. We drove from the house early in the morning by car. My husband was driving and I was busy with our son who was 13 months old and he just started saying some words in Arabic. The plan was to stay one week in Jordan and Palestine to visit the Holy Land.

It was close to getting through the Iraqi boarder, in order to get clearance to get into Jordan that took about 6 hours. There was a long line of cars and trucks all trying to cross the boarder at R'waished/ Traibil. After clearing our papers and passports we drove through the desert. Driving through the desert took a long time and lots of dust.

After we drove off the Iraqi boarder and continued into Jordan's again long hours of driving in the desert until we arrived in Amman, the capital of Jordan.

The first hotel we came to my husband stopped to stay in for the night and rest. It was a long drive and boring through the desert with no view to enjoy. We were so tired that we fell asleep until the waking call came from the front desk as we requested. My husband right away ordered breakfast and milk for Faris our son. After we took a shower, we packed and were ready to hit the road to the Holy Land (Jerusalem) that was a few hours away.

It was a great trip this time. We drove through Jordon where we spent a week visiting the Holy land and stayed in Jerusalem. It was safe at that time and our hotel was near the border with Israel. We used to see the Palestinian soldiers talking to the Israeli soldiers.

We arrived to the Holy Land-Jerusalem by noon. After we found the right hotel with a beautiful view facing the mountains and the other side facing a large field with a high wall, we learned the other side was Israel. On those days, we Iraqi's were not able to visit Israel. Otherwise we will be in a bad situation with the Iraqi government. Remember; this is part of the Holy land was occupied by the Palestinians.

After we were situated and relaxed, we went out for a walk to check out the area and also to eat lunch. We needed to gather information about the Holy land and visit the village where Jesus was born and the city was called (Bethlehem).

Walking through the city of Jerusalem, there was a gate from the old city, which had two lions on the top. The gate, we learned later on was broken by the Jews when they occupied the area. The streets were very narrow. We visited the church St. Ann's Mary's mother) that was built by the crusaders'. It was a long day with our baby, so we went back to the hotel to relax and we planned to visit other places the next day.

We started with Mount Olive, the Garden of Gethsemane, where Jesus spent his last hours praying before he was arrested. There were so many splendid churches in this sacred place. We visited the Grotto of Agony, which was not far from The Tomb of the Virgin Mary. We also visited the trail of the way of the cross.

We visited the street that was called the route of Suffering. The Church of Holy Sepulcher was built on the land where Jesus was crucified and buried and was risen after the third-day. According to some people we were told that in 1948, after World War II, the Jordanian took Jerusalem, and later the Israelis in 1967, took back the city.

We needed to explore Ramallah, where most of the Palestinians lived after the Israeli occupation. It was a small village, clean and safe.

The last day we had to visit the Jordan River, where John the Baptist baptized Jesus Christ. This biblical river, which has inspired countless spiritual people, is just a narrow stream in many parts.

It was at the southern Jordan River, that the Bible say, that the people of Israel crossed into the Promised Land. And in its waters, Christians believe Jesus was baptized. It was also said that the Jordan River passes the Dead Sea

We then left the area to go back to the hotel to rest. Our plan for the next morning was to leave to Beirut-Lebanon. The next day, we left after breakfast as planned. Our next stop was Damascus the Capital of Syria.

The Road to Beirut

We are going to Beirut two years later, after spending our honeymoon in Lebanon. Great memories came to my mind. This time we have our car and we don't need anyone to take care of us.

The road to Beirut was great with beautiful green mountains without the desert. There were farmers along the roads selling fruits and vegetables freshly cut from their garden. We stopped to get some fruits as we were thirsty and then we stopped at a restaurant that had the best rotisserie chicken. Then we headed to the house on the mountain that we rented to stay for the summer season.

We arrived at the house and the lady of the house was waiting for us. She started welcoming us, trying to make us feel comfortable and she wanted to accommodate our one-year-son. She brought him home cooked food to eat since she has a year old son herself.

The Lebanese usually rent their homes in the summer season for tourists to generate income and they live in a small garage adjacent to their house. Lebanon's economy is always dependent on tourism since the country had no dependable jobs for the residence. My husband talked to the lady asking which are the best stores to shop at. She was very helpful in making her recommendations.

My husband stared taking down the luggage, and I had to put my son in the crib. I needed to relax myself as I was tired.

The next day we un-packed the luggage and my husband went shopping for groceries. I gave a bath to my one-year-old son and fed him and put him to sleep. I sat on the balcony facing the mountains, looking down to the valley. Lebanon is blessed with beautiful, natural resources.

Lebanon is located on the Mediterranean Sea with the best fresh seafood and land on the mountains is fertile. All the vegetables and fruits that might be seasonal in different countries, but in Lebanon they will be available year round. In size Lebanon is small, but high mountains makes it large in size.

The valleys plant fruits and vegetables for that weather and on the top of the mountains the plants for clod and snowy weather and you will see all that in all seasons. [I remember in Beirut for my honeymoon, Beirut was hot and humid in April and when my grand father came to take us to his house on the mountain we were surprised to find snow on the side of the road and on the mountains.]

I was waiting for my husband and fell asleep next to my son when I heard and knock on the door. I ran to open it and was surprised to see my aunt. She said to me the people in town remember you as a bride and they want to come and see you. I invited her in and made coffee for us to drink.

When my husband came he was shocked how the whole town knew about our arrival. He said that they all remembered him and wanted to see the baby and me. My aunt suggested to us to attend church on Sunday to be able to see everyone. We agreed.

That evening, we went to visit my grandfather and my aunts. We had a good time and that was the first time to see my son. My son Faris was the first great grand son. We enjoyed the attention from the family, as well as people who lived in Falougha.

Jeita Grotto

We had a car that allowed us to visit most of the sight seeing, the ones that were recommended places to the tourists. One of the Seven Wonders of nature Jeita Grotto,

These caves can be visited only by boat, inside the mountain that has Karstic limestone Caves and was discovered in1836.

We were on our way to Jeita grotto. As we arrived at the sight, we looked around and asked the tour company about the arrangements. We were lucky it was not crowded with tourists, so we took our time.

We were excited to take the tour, and my husband was paying for the paddleboat that will take us through the caves. As we were ready to take the boat, security stopped us telling us that we cannot take our son with us. We looked at each other speechless wondering what are we going to do. I was afraid to go by myself and, we were negotiating. Here was an old Lebanese man sitting on the side and he offered to keep an eye on our son.

We looked at each other thinking the same thing, 'how could we trust a man we do not know"? Right away the security man knew what was going on and right away he said to my husband that they were brothers and have children of their own, and they will take good care of our baby.

We were convinced and we left our son with them in his car seat. The tour took 30 minutes that seemed to me like three hours I did not enjoy the boat ride and I was busy praying most of the time. In those days people can be trusted, but we took a chance. Thanks God, when we came back our son was where we left him, safe and sleeping.

This incident reminded me of my childhood. I was about seven years old when my grandfather took all of us grandchildren to the park. There were 8 children. We were four, and my cousins were four similar ages since my mother and her sister had children at the same time. We were three sisters and fourth brother was 3 years old, riding his tricycle. We had a great time and when the sun started going down, my grandfather took us all to the car and we got into our seats and headed home. When we were home and our mothers came to get us of the car, I heard my mom screaming and crying my brother was missing.

Immediately, my grandfather went back to the park and found out that the gate was chained and locked. Without delay, he headed to the police station informing them that he believes that his grandson is still in the park. Right away the police called the park security and found out that my brother was safe, with the security guy knowing that the parents will come back for their son. My grandfather and the police drove together to the park and picked up my brother. My mother was still crying when her dad came back with her baby son.

After Jeita Grotto we went to down town Beirut to have dinner. We were happy that we got to see and visit the Jeita and the same time our son was safe. We continued sight seeing. Lebanon is great, you can be at the beach swimming in the morning and leave to the mountains to ski or go snowboarding. At night they have the best casinos and entertainment.

We walked through the town, and by now we have met most of the people. Everyone knew who we were and would greet us and invite us to his or her homes. We also visited my grandfather's house, since he always has visitors either from the neighboring towns or out of the country visitors.

We visited every site that we needed to visit and had good time. We did a lot of shopping since Lebanon had a free market and were connected to the European markets.

On our way to Lebanon via Syria, we stayed there all day and we shopped and we headed directly to Lebanon. Lebanon is great in the summer, especially on the mountains, since Beirut is hot and humid.

We enjoyed socializing with my grandfather, his visitors, and friends in town. The town remembered us from the time we spent there for our honeymoon. We had an idea to immigrate at that time and my husband was looking in the newspaper for jobs in the States. However, his family did not encourage him and wanted us to get back to Baghdad

(R'waished/Jordan) at the boarder of (Traibil /Iraq)

These caves can be visited only by row inside the
mountain that has Karstic limestone Caves.

Chapter 24

Coming back to Baghdad

Our 4 months vacation in Lebanon was great. Thinking of staying in Baghdad was stressful after the long drive from Lebanon through Syria, where they gave us a hard time because we had shopped from Lebanon. We know that Syria did not like tourists to, spend their vacations in Lebanon, verses Syria.

We went back to Basra to bring our youngest son who was taken care of by my mom and his nanny. We stayed a few days in Basra with the family and friends. Then we went back to Baghdad. By then, my husband's sister was engaged and married to her cousin who happened to be visiting Iraq from the United States.

We encouraged her to marry her cousin and they had their wedding celebration in Baghdad, followed by a trip to Europe for their honeymoon. After she settled in the States she sent letters informing us that she enjoys her life in the States. Since her husband is an American citizen, she will be eligible to have her own citizenship after three years.

After my husband's company was nationalized he was not comfortable to work there and we were looking for a way to leave the country. We knew that the opportunity is getting close since his sister is married to her cousin who happened to be an American citizen, which means that she will become a citizen in three years.

My husband felt the pressure on me with two children and his mother and sister never helped and restricted our freedom in the home. Then to make things worse, his older brother who lost his job in Germany, came back to live with us.

The situation deteriorated between all of us, it was obvious. My husband's family teamed up on us, hoping for us to move out of the house. I felt the pressure and my husband's because he felt that the house was his father's inheritance for the whole family. He resisted the move since he was the youngest and was taking care of his mother and the older sisters when his older brother left them and went to Germany.

Few years later, his brother came back from Germany with his pregnant wife who forced him to return to Baghdad to be close to her family. It was not easy to live with all these people at that house. So we planned to move out.

Moving to our own home

To end the pressure and constant stressful atmosphere, I convinced my husband to move out for our own insanity. Finally, we sent the nanny back to her parents after I bought her lots of clothes. She was happy to go back to her village. At last we moved out, rented our own home, and furnished it with modern furniture to fit our lifestyle. The garden was large and the children were happy and had their freedom to play around.

Our neighbors were great from both sides. One side we had older family friendly and sociable with us. On the other side there were older couple with teenage children. The children loved my boys and they took them to their house to play with them and sometimes I used them to baby sat for my children. I felt comfortable for the arrangements because I knew that my boys were taken care of and are enjoying the other children.

> *"in the end, you'll know which people really love you. They are the ones who see you for who you are and no matter what, and they always will find a way to be at your side."* ~Unknown Quotes ~

Our lifestyle changed we had lots of friends in Baghdad and visited my family in Basra. We enjoyed socializing and we visited my aunt and uncle they lived two blocks away from us. Sometimes we visited them after we put the kids to sleep. We would talk to the children that we are not far away just visiting the neighbors.

After few months we started thinking about leaving the country. We began planning. It took us few years to prepare ourselves for the move. We had to keep everything to ourselves and were working hard on the move. We had to be patient for my husband's sister to become American citizen for her to be able to process our immigration papers under the family reunification immigration act.

Meanwhile we kept our life going normally so that people will not suspect of anything going on. We visited my parents occasionally especially during the Holidays and the children visited their grandmother.

My husband started feeling the pressure from management. Since he was the top sales manager he used to meet with the company's head quarters quarterly. My husband always kept a low profile he wanted to kill time until we are ready to leave the country.

Our neighbors knew that my family is in Basra and we visit them all the time especially during holidays. My husband started working to complete our passports and the children's passports. He also applied for a vacation time. His manager said to him joking" I hope that you are not leaving the country for good." My husband denied the manager's comment and he stated that he is going to Basra to visit my parents.

I was busy with my fiends and close relatives in Baghdad, and my husband was busy in his job. He did not travel on the job as before which made me happy for him to spend more time with the children and me. We enjoyed doing sight seeing in Baghdad we visited Baghdad International Airport and the children enjoyed watching the planes landing and taking off.

We visited the amusement park that the children enjoyed getting in rides that fit their age. We took them to a petting zoo. The most they enjoyed was the airport watching the planes taking off. They loved sitting in the swimming pool that their aunt sent them from the states.

Iraq then was peaceful and life was normal. However we felt that the country is taking a bad turn since my husband's company was nationalized and he was unhappy at work, he knew that things would not go back to normal.

Chapter 25

Preparing to move to the States:

> *"This is about Faith, courage and commitment to*
> *achieve the American Dream."*
> *My parents should have come to the United stated*
> *when my father was granted immigration visa (through*
> *a quota system that he had applied for when he was*
> *single). I was not born the time and my father wanted to*
> *continue with his plan to proceed with the immigration*
> *process but my mother refused to do so because she did*
> *not want to leave her parents and siblings*
> *~Salma Ajo, Author~*

After we had our first son, my husband's company was nationalized among other companies that were owned and/or managed by foreigners. My husband was not comfortable for the changes. It was not good change.

In 1970, my husband began to feel political pressures at work. He was uncomfortable with the fact that workers of the Baath's party were encouraged to spy on each other. There were widespread disturbing changes everywhere. One day my husband came home from work; I noticed he was not the same. Then he told me that his manager had acquired a list of names of his co-workers with their political affiliation link.

I saw my husband was in a double bind. If my husband complied with the firing orders, he would betray his co-workers, and if he did not then his job and his life were in jeopardy. My husband himself was never involved politically. As he was talking, my thoughts were searching for answers to our dilemma. Suddenly, I said to him, "Let's go to America." He agreed, saying that the same thought had crossed his mind, but he was afraid I might not be in favor of the idea. We were both ready for the move.

Both of us had a similar educational and multilingual backgrounds were very encouraging to take the next step. My husband was educated at the American Jesuit priests in school and college in Baghdad. I had my education at the French Dominican sisters in Basra. Arabic was the main language, however, the concentration was more on the English and French languages and my studies of English in India in an Irish School with Irish and Germen nuns. With our language background, we knew we were well prepared for the change.

We were young and determined that nothing was going to get in our way. We came to realize that our country was going through an intensive political regime in which we did not wish to be part of.

Finally, our decision was made to move on. We decided to immigrate to the United States. Our intention was to have his sister who was American Citizen to sponsor us according to the immigration law of "Family Reunification Act". We were ready to face any challenges that came our way. We planned our move very carefully.

My husband started preparing and updating all our documents and our legal papers that we need to get our passports with the all the documents that was necessary to present to the American Embassy including our birth certificates, Baptism papers, passports, legal clarifications documents for my husband and myself and extra pictures.

We decided not to tell our families until we are ready to leave. We did not want to let anyone about what was going on. It was difficult during our first step in the move. However, we were eager and determined to leave and promised ourselves not to look back. We were ready for a fresh start.

The first step was to visit the American Embassy. During that time direct diplomatic relations between Iraq and the United States were frozen. The closest American Embassy was in Kuwait. Kuwait is only a two-hour drive from my hometown, Basra. In spite of travel restriction on government employees, we managed to take advantage of the Muslim Holiday to travel to Kuwait. We had been advised that the American Embassy was being watched by the Iraqi secret service for Iraqi males who visited the Embassy. Iraqi females were not of any concern.

In September 1969, the plan was to visit my parents in Basra and then drive to Kuwait for a few days. On my first visit to the American Embassy, my husband dropped me off with all the documents required for the immigration visa. As I entered the American Embassy I had a powerful and strong feelings of anxiety and fear. After I talked to the secretary that was very polite and she seemed to notice that I was anxious. She started calming me down saying be not afraid. We talked and she said to me that I should be very comfortable going to the stated with my English Language it will be easier for me and my family.

The American Embassy secretary told me that the process would not take long, rather few months. My answer to her was do not call us we will be back soon. We were excited about making the connection and the first move. Our timing was perfect.

On the way back to Basra my husband and I decided to keep everything hush-hush from everyone including our parents and family. During those days the Iraqi government did not allow travel to the United States. Iraqi passports were stamped "Travel is permitted all over the world except Israel and America." However when applied for the new passports the restrictions were "permitted only to the Arab Countries.

Our plan had to be kept secret. We did not want to deal with our parents as well. To them, America seemed to be so far away. We were very excited. We started planning our future in America. The plan was to get one-way tickets to the United States. My husband as a government employ was to get a special vacation order to Lebanon when he asked his supervisor for vacation consent to visit his sick brother. We remained as careful and secretive as possible and not to allow anyone to suspect us of leaving the country. We knew that if the government suspected we would be restricted from leaving the country and possible jailed time.

And so I tell you, keep on asking, and you will receive -
What you ask for. Keep on asking, and you will find. Keep
on knocking, and the door will be opened for you.
~ LUKE 11:9 NLT ~

Our second visit to the American Embassy in Kuwait occurred during Christmas vacation. While visiting my parents in Basra, I asked my mother to watch the children during our visit so that we can go to Kuwait for shopping. My husband and I made our second visit to the American Embassy. The secretary surprised me by saying that our visas were ready. I told her that we were not ready yet. We needed to go back to Baghdad and sell the house and furniture before leaving. I asked the secretary to keep the papers ready and promised her that we would be back in a month to leave for the United States.

I left the American Embassy so happy not believing how easy the process was. As soon as I sat in the car and told my husband he kept asking me to make sure that I understood right. We were on a pink cloud returning to Basra trying to plan for the next step.

Now was a difficult timing. We decided to break the news to my parents. They were shocked and tried to give us advice about how hard it would be to relocate to another country, especially with young children. My father was happy and he encouraged me in an indirect way and for the first time he mentioned that he had wanted to leave for the United States before I was born, but my mother did not want to leave her family. They never discussed the subject again.

In Baghdad, we had no choice but to inform my husband's family. They were surprised and did not believe that we were really serious. We managed to sell the house, and we left with our personal belongings (four suitcases). We told the neighbors and the people who bought the house that my husband had been transferred to Basra and that we were going to live with my parents. Our real plan was to spend a few days with my family, say our good byes to my family and friends, proceed toward our last stop, Kuwait and to the American Embassy to pick up our entry visas to the United States.

During those days, immigration quotas were newly reformed which made our immigration process quick and easy. The city of Basra is where I grew up. It is the port of Iraq and geographically located on the border of Kuwait.

We couldn't believe how easy it was getting the immigration visa. Today, it takes approximately 10-15 years for the same visa due to restricting immigration reform laws.

Things were happening so fast that I was not able to think clearly about what it means to leave one's country and familiar surroundings.

Regardless of mixed feelings, we were determined to leave. We left the city of Baghdad on February 15, 1971, and traveled to Basra where my parents lived where we spent two days with them. Then we travelled to Kuwait for my husband to complete all the papers, and the medical and physical evaluation by an assigned physician by the American Embassy.

My husband had booked our plane tickets with the Czechoslovakian airlines since he had a friend who worked there and issued for us one-way tickets from Kuwait to New York. The plan was for my husband to leave Kuwait, making a stop at Prague, Czechoslovakia for 3 days and continue to London with a stay of 4 days. Next was to aboard another plane with another ticket to New York, then proceed to with a connection flight to Detroit.

After completing all the papers the visas were ready to be picked up the day we would leave Kuwait. My husband left Kuwait right away and I went with my father back to Basra to leave in two weeks. My husband said to me "stay longer with your family. You might not see them again." I was miserable in Basra without my husband. I was not able to tell people that I was leaving the country for good. I was frightened and worried. I visited the church and was praying to be safe and join my husband.

> *Sit back relax and let God take the steering wheel.*
> *I guarantee He'll take you to places you couldn't even*
> *dream of."*
> ~Unknown~

When the time came to leave and said my goodbye to my family, it was very hard but I was looking forward to join my husband and settle down. I left Basra with my father and my two infant children two days prior to my flight schedule. It was dark in the evening when the taxicab stopped at the boarder between Basra and Kuwait ad a checkpoint in a small town called Safwan.

My dad and the taxicab driver went to see the officer to show our passports and visa to enter Kuwait. They were delayed and I was praying, I had feeling that something is going to happen. My dad came to the car and said to me that the officer wants to see me. I got off the car with my children shivering with fear what is awaiting me.

The officer asked me few questions about my intention to enter Kuwait. I told him that I would be catching a flight to Europe to be with my husband. He explained to me the reason he questioned me because my visa stated that I was going to stay at the Sheraton Hotel. I explained to him that I was planning to come with my cousin and her husband and he applied for my visa. The officer seemed to be satisfied and was OK with my answers, stamped our passports and let us cross the boarder to Kuwait.

It hit me later on. I was supposed to go to Kuwait with my cousin and her husband and my visa stated that we were to stay in the Sheraton Hotel. Then they cancelled and my dad accompanied me with the children. Later on my dad explained to me that single women were not allowed to enter Kuwait alone to minimize prostitution. I thanked God that the officer was not mean to make too much of the issue.

The next morning I was to go to the American Embassy to pick up our immigration papers and visa to enter New York. Our flight was one am after mid night that day. I woke up early changed and left the boys with an Iraqi lady that my dad had rented an apartment from her since he was working in Kuwait. The lady was very helpful she called for me a cab driver that she assured me he is very responsible and family man that she knew to take me to the American Embassy.

I arrived the Embassy signed my name and took a seat waiting my turn. After about one hour the secretary called me and said to me "I am sorry it seems that your medical file is missing". I was scared and tearful trying to make her understand that I have to take that night the flight since that specific airline takes passengers from Kuwait twice a week only and I cannot stay three more days that will loose my connection in Czechoslovakia.

The secretary asked me if I knew the doctor that I did the physical at. I said to her that my husband was with me and everything was done before he left. The lady was kind and understanding when I mentioned to her that I had left my two children were a lady waiting for me.

She started looking around and talked to some people and finally called me and said there is two Iraqi men one of them is also leaving to the States to join his wife and children and he used the same physician that I used and they are willing to take me to the doctor's office to pick up my papers. The secretary promised me that she would wait for me until we come back. I believe she sensed that I was scared.

I had no choice but go along with these two strangers in a foreign country not know what is going to happen to me and I might never see my children and my husband again. I introduced myself to them and thanked them in advance for doing this favor to me.

It was a small two-door Volkswagen car. I took the back seat and started praying to stay safe and these people will not hurt me. I found out that the driver lives in Kuwait and the other guy is his friend staying with him until his visa is ready. The drive took about one hour. By the time we reached the doctor's office, there was a sign on the door stating that the clinic is closed for lunch and they will be back at 2:00 pm.

Although this incident happened more than thirty years ago, the memories are so vivid and crystal-clear that I am experiencing the same tingling emotional sensation mixed with ambiguity of fear doubting these individuals whether they are good or bad people. I promised myself and my God that I will stay in my seat emotionally devastated, worried about myself I do not know where I am but at the mercy of those two strangers.

While I was in my own world, trying to figure out what is happening and how can I get out of this dilemma. I heard one of them saying to me that the apartment is close by and we could stop there to cool down from the heat of the desert to have some cold beverages. My answer to them was going ahead I would stay in the car. I knew deep inside me that there is no way anyone to move me from my seat until I get to the doctor's office.

They kept on trying each from different direction but I was quite. They even started making sexual advances where the one who is leaving to the states said to me that the two of us have missed our spouses and this was a good chance to have some fun. I was so angry but yet I decided to ignore him and I was quite and my prayers made me stronger. Finally time was close to 1:00 pm and we were on our way to the doctors' office.

I believe in faith and trust in God and he is the only one that will take me safe back to my husband and children. I was counting the minutes that seemed like hours to get back home. We arrived at the doctor's office and the nurse said to me to wait to make the packet since she was to run more copies. I thanked her appreciatively and waited anxiously to get all the required papers assuring her not to forget anything. After one hour I was handed the papers and we were on our way to the American Embassy. I was praying all the way that the secretary would be waiting for me. We run into the rush hour and people leaving work.

Upon our arrival to the Embassy, the secretary was waiting for me and after I handed her the medical report, she completed the package and she took it added the immigration papers sealed it and handed to me instructing me to give it to the immigration personal when arriving New York where they will issue us our green cards.

I thanked her and she asked the two Iraqi's to take me home. I was shaking out of fear and the secretary asked me for the address stating that she would like to make a photocopy. I had the address gave it to her to make a copy for her and I gave them my copy and asked her to call the phone # and let my dad know that I am on my way. I believe she understood why I wanted her to do so since I cannot trust the two guys. I felt somehow relaxed knowing that I was just minutes for me to be uniting with my children and my father.

As we approached the house, I saw my dad and the lady each of them carrying the two children and they seemed worry about me. My tears came down thanking God finally I am home with them. As I thanked the guys, trying not to let my dad suspect that I was upset and scared trying to explain to my dad how they lost the papers at the Embassy and we had to go to the doctor to get copies of all the documents.

I went inside the house and put the boys in bed until time to catch our flight the same night. I prepared the luggage and the plane tickets and the immigration papers in a small carry-on bag to be safe with me all the time. When time was close to leave to the airport, my dad had arrange for a taxi cab to pick us up and he came with us to make sure that we will be on the flight on time.

Finally the plane left Kuwait after mid-night non-stop to land in Prague Czechoslovakia. It was a long journey. The plane landed at Prague the next morning and we were able to pick up the bus to the hotel.

Prague/Czechoslovakia

Arriving to the hotel, I was surprise to find the two Iraqi families with us going to the United States/Detroit, Michigan. They were very friendly and we started sharing our stories of leaving Iraq. They started helping me with the children and I was helping them with the language and we were able to communicate with the hotel receptionists. I was relaxed and thanked God that there will be no more surprises.

I had one surprise when went to register at the hotel's front desk I found out that I my husband had left me a letter at the hotel with the necessary arrangement and how to get around in Prague and the best place to exchange the money was at the hotel. I shared the information with the other families.

The other families were happy to see me more outgoing and we went shopping together by taking the train that started on the circle across from the hotel entrance. We spent three days and had great time together. We went shopping and sightseeing by staying in the train. I was shocked to find out people on the bus were not able to speak English even College students. It was a fun trip.

By the fourth day we woke up early to catch our plane to the states with one stop was in Montreal Canada. We were ready to leave the hotel to the airport to take our flight to New York.

Chapter 26

Arriving to the States

> *"If you choose to place your happiness on external factors,
> you will be constantly searching for that next "want."
> Yet, if you place your happiness on what lives inside of
> you, you'll be able to find contentment and peace of
> mind."*
> *-Michelle Sedas, Inspired Living Center-*

Arrived in the United States, at LaGuardia Airport when I found out that the connecting flight from New York to Detroit was on strike and we were to take another connecting plane. By this time I lost the other family since they were with the immigration officers to process our entry visa and the Green cards for the children and myself.

I took my children heading to the airport exist. We needed find a way to get to John F. Kennedy Airport. Suddenly I heard my name was called, as I looked around I found my husband's cousin who left Iraq few months before we did. He came toward us making room for himself pushing the crowed to get closer to us. After greeting each other he informed me that my husband had called him to pick us up from this airport and take us to the other airport to take the plane to Detroit since our plane was on strike. I was finally relaxed and I was close to join my husband.

We arrived Detroit Metropolitan airport on my husband' Birthday, March 8, 1971. My husband and his sister were there to pick us up.

Finally I joined my husband and we stayed two weeks with my husband's sister. Living in somebody else's home was uncomfortable. Our privacy was limited and our children's movements were restricted. We were lucky, my husband found work and after a few weeks we were able to locate a small apartment and we moved in.

My husband had already bought himself a brand new car. By the time my husband paid the down payment on the car he needed, and made the apartment deposit, we had depleted most of our money and could only afford a few pieces of furniture.

My husband was laid-off after two weeks of work. I found a job as a seamstress at a bridal shop and started working. We were very happy and doing our best to adjust to our new life. We budgeted our money; it was fun to monitor our spending. We have never budgeted our spending. We knew before we came to America that there were going to get through difficult times, but we were young, ambitious and had endurance and promised ourselves to accept whatever comes along.

I was paid a minimum wage. Half of my salary was going for taxes and babysitting, but I kept working because we needed every penny. I must admit it was not easy to arrive in a country with a completely different culture and no family members from my side of the family. My husband's sister was not supportive of our coming to the States. In spite of everything we refused to hold onto negative feelings about our experiences. We were happy to accept whatever the future was to offer us. We decided to make things work and concentrated on our future. We wanted to prove to our families that we made the right choice.

Soon after our arrival my husband found a good job as a salesman for a company who supplied food for restaurants as a salesman with a good salary plus commission. He also was furnished with a brand new personal car and health insurance for the whole family.

I was able to quit my job and stay with the boys since it was summer vacation. My husband worked hard. He worked three jobs at one time. Our acquaintance with the English language helped us. We promised ourselves we would not look back. We were determined to succeed.

My husband was happy with his job, but he was still looking for another part time job that he could do in the evening. One day, as he was reading the newspaper, he found what he thought he was looking for. He contacted the company's owner, an engineer who manufactured garbage bags and needed a salesman to take orders and he would deliver them. The agreement was that my husband would pick up the orders and call the manufacturer with the orders to be delivered, and then he would send my husband with the commission check.

This was a second job for my husband besides the restaurant food company. My husband was working hard to get the orders and forwarded them to the manufacturer. We were not the only ones that were surprised at the response of the retailers. The manufacturer could not keep up with the production. We were receiving big checks twice a week. We couldn't believe what was happening. My husbands said to me, "That's what they call the 'land of opportunity'." This business activity lasted for six months until the manufacturer couldn't make daily deliveries and asked my husband's help.

My husband knew of a man who owned a warehouse and he might be interested to be involved in the business deal. My husband made the deal to use the warehouse for certain fees, not knowing that he would be double-crossed by the warehouse owner. The manufacturer was even greedier and made his dealings directly with the warehouse owner. To make a long story short the warehouse owner could not sell the merchandise and the manufacturer couldn't make his payments so he ended up filing bankruptcy.

I believe that hard work; determination and commitment brought us luck and fortune. Looking back, we were both the kind of people who exerted ourselves. Ambitious is the exact word that applies to us. When I am talking about success, it is not the money that is associated with success. I mean the self-respect and self-satisfaction that are the results of hard work. I believe that's why we immigration to the United States "for a better appreciation of life." Very quickly, my husband learned the business well enough to form his own wholesale corporation

I believe that in recalling our circumstances I have discovered the critical moments connected with my immigration experience. I have discovered many hidden feelings that I have ignored. Within me is a passionate curiosity to explore and reveal the essential features of my experience during the time I left my home country. I truly can feel my heart beat and my tears coming as I write my experience of the immigration process.

Yes, there were losses but I have been compensated for them in rich and rewarding ways. I believe that I have made a good choice in adopting the United States as my country. I became an American citizen on July 4, 1977 (the Bicentennial year). One does not choose the country of one's birth, but I am proud to say I became a citizen of the United Stated by choice.

After I became a citizen, my husband and I discussed the issue of taking the children to Iraq to visit his mother since she was getting old and we thought it was a good timing for her to see them. I made a visit to the passport department in downtown to apply for American Passports for myself the two boys who were born in Iraq and the youngest that is American by birth.

Upon on our arrival to the office to apply for the passports, the officer brought to my attention a letter posted on the wall and asked me to read it before I sign the application. Basically it read as: If you were a a citizen of one of these countries listed below, we advise you not to go, and if you go, then you are on your own risk." The countries that were listed in the flyer were: all the Arab countries, Turkey, Iran, and Greece.

After I was done reading the flyer, the officer asked me is I was still interested to get our passports. My answer was "yes". I completed the application process and returned home. I mentioned that to my husband he did not take it seriously. A week later a large package came in the mail with our American passports. I was excited; there was a copy of the flyer that I saw at the office with every passport except in my American born son his passport had nothing attached to it.

When my husband came home from work, I informed him about the arrival of the passports and he was excited but soon his excitement diminished after he read the flyer and said to me; "no one will go at this time, this is a very serious situation. There is something going on now or in the near future that's why they don't want anyone to travel to these countries." I accepted the situation but I was disappointed at the same time.

A letter from your Immigrant Parents

I dedicate this letter to my three boys, Faris, Mahir and Ramzi Jr., and to all the children of immigrants that are labeled the second generation. This letter is also addressed to each one of you, from your "immigrant parents."

Dear son,

Better life conditions forced us to immigrate to the United States of America. Separation from friends and family was not easy. America may be a nationalist, non-civil, racially prejudiced country today, yet you did not experience the challenges that faced first generation immigrants such as language barriers that cause alienation, loneliness and isolation. However, your determination and hard work came from our overcoming hurdles in just coming to America.

When I am challenged I feel stronger. Being a first generation immigrant I feel I was always challenged, even raising you in a completely different culture and under different conditions. When you were young you were great. You listened unconditionally, "mom is always right." However, growing up, the conflict between the old culture and the new American way of life was pulling you in opposite directions. We as first generation immigrant parents realize that our need was for freedom and stability, while you are looking for your personal satisfaction; you have lived "within bits and pieces of two countries, the mixture aiding to fuse and confuse us all the more."

You need to realize that we (your immigrant parents) have been displaced from family, land, customs, and expectations in the old country (Iraq), they literally died from the move. However, the emotional suffering on you may have been as intense. We are sure that sometimes you felt different from your peers and that created anxiety, fear and anger within you, thus your diversity added a unique quality to your character. However, we are glad you were always proud of your origin. Other sons lost identity and denied or changed names and altered faces. Today, I see other sons who defy the elders, and have lost the sense of family tradition in the name of being Americanized; some developed poor habits practiced by American teens including unprotected sex, drug and alcohol abuse.

Through my early practice with immigrants, I have observed a generational gap that caused conflict between parents and their American raised children. Immigrant parents and their children see the world differently and have developed different conceptions of social reality. These differences sometimes threaten their relationships.

As you were growing up, you were always happy and caring for each other, which I highly encourage you to keep--especially family unity. You learned to respect and be proud of each other as well as keep the cultural values. Thus you were accustomed to the American life and I was proud of you. Baseball teams and Boy Scout expeditions, summer vacation camps gave you the sense of being American. Enjoy the American life and the American friends but do not forget your background and your culture. Take the best out of the two cultures to keep and act upon. Do not break away from your culture--contribute back. Be proud of who you are and from where your parents came, and most of all pass your memories and knowledge of your history to your children. Remember the old Arabic saying, "He who denies his roots stays wobbly."

Our success came from hard work and appreciation of America that opened the doors for us. For years after we emigrated, I questioned myself--if we did the right thing for you bringing you to America. However, after the Iran-Iraq war and the Gulf War, I thanked God that we made the move when you were very young. I feel that we made the best choice ever and I ask you in return to maintain the pride we have for you always.

Oh, yes--we wanted freedom and security and we want you to have that too and enjoy life in "Great America."

Your Loving Mom,

Salma Ajo, Ph.D.

Chapter 27

Yes, many immigrants cherish the value of choice and
opportunity and the value of education more than
7th or 8th generation Americans.
~Malcolm Wallop~

Living in the States

Arriving to the States I felt I was ready to face new challenges and beyond. The sumounting of our earlier difficulties in life had made us into stronger human beings, able to rely largely on our own individual resources and to support each other well.

I believe that hard work and determination brought us luck and fortune. Looking back, we were both the kind of people who exerted ourselves to succeed and get ahead. Ambitious is the exact word that applies to us. When I am talking about success, it is not the money that is associated with success. I mean the self-respect and self-satisfaction that are the results of hard work. I believe that's why we immigrated to the United States "for a better appreciation of life."

Since the time I immigrated to the United States, I kept busy accommodating my family's needs first, and then others who needed help. I was fortunate that when I immigrated my English skills were not limited. Helping people was a big challenge in my life.

I believe that in recalling our circumstances I have discovered the critical moments connected with my immigration experience. I have discovered many hidden feelings that I have ignored. Within me is a passionate curiosity to explore and reveal the essential features of my experience during the time I left my home country. I truly can feel it in my heartbeat and my tears coming as I write my experience of the immigration process.

We were blessed with a third son Ramzi Jr. after a year in the United States. The boys were thrilled to have a new baby brother. My husband was so excited that he named him after himself. I realized that my husband was building a future from scratch and my job was to take care of the children. I had reached a level of maturity that led me to enjoy and become close to my children.

I was busy with my children and was not aware of being a stranger in a strange country. I adapted myself to the environment.

I had no time to feel lonely, though, at times I felt homesick. I longed to be with my parents and siblings. However, my husband and children filled the emptiness in my life; they and my new life filled my life.

Yes, there were losses but I have been compensated for them in rich and rewarding ways believing that I have made a good choice in adopting the United States as my country. I became an American citizen on July 4, 1977 (the Bicentennial year). One does not choose the country of one's birth, but I am proud to say I became a citizen of the United Stated by choice.

I loved our Chaldean culture. Although I tried to pass the culture to my children, they received it differently. Faris my oldest son, loves being a Chaldean and he would correct anyone that would mispronounce his name. He likes his name to be pronounced exactly the way we say it. Unlike Mahir, who uses "Mikey" when he is around his American friends. As for Ramzi Jr., he loves being an American-born. All the boys love being in America.

I read voraciously and was very curious about learning new things in books, on television, and by attending school functions. In 1975, an adult education program started at a neighborhood school. I was excited and told my husband I wanted to finish high school. Although he did not encourage me, I registered anyway. The school had a free babysitting service for my youngest son. The older boys were already in school. The plan worked for me to attend adult education and my son was taken care of.

While I attended high school classes, I was introduced to my first psychology course. I enjoyed the course and developed an extraordinary interest in the subject. I started reading books related to psychology. I did so well that the instructor did not believe it was my first introduction to psychology. I began to notice that psychological studies were natural for me.

Perhaps having lived in several cultures enhanced my ability to understand different personalities. I learned not to be judgmental, to respect others' opinions, and to accept them. The values I learned from my parents and my education in Iraq added to my competencies. I do not remember being introduced to discrimination, hate, or prejudice. I believe that this universal regard for all others shaped my life and helped me develop long lasting relationships and love for people of varied race, color and ethnicity.

I completed the high school program in two years. I wanted to attend college, but my husband did not agree. He justified his position: "Your life is secure and you do not need to work to support yourself." His other reason was that the children were too young and needed my undivided attention.

We argued and the issue came between us, causing conflicts. He was so firm in his decision that I knew I had to choose between my marriage and education. As usual, I prayed a lot to receive help from God and get His guidance to make the right decision. Although I longed for more intellectual stimulation, I believe that my decision helped me to make the right decision by choosing my marriage.

Years passed and I was busy with the children. After I became a citizen, I applied for my parents for emigration to the United States through the family re-unification law. At that time the process was very easy and quick.

Although I managed to compromise with others in the family, I frequently reminded my husband that I wanted to obtain a college degree. I helped others fill out applications for work and volunteered my time to various organizations. I was busy between volunteering and helping my family and friends.

My husband encouraged me to take the children on trips because he was occupied with his business. He wanted me to be more independent. His ideas were different from other Chaldean men. He was and still is liberal in his thinking. He trusted me and wanted me to have the best.

He is always attentive and realistic to the family's future. He wanted me to have my independence by appointing me as the treasurer in the corporation. He motivated me to establish my own checking account and obtain my own credit cards.

His motive was clear. He wanted me to be able to control the business if anything happened to him. He was different in his thinking. Chaldean husbands usually try to control and keep the wife in the dark. (This was 40 years ago. Women today are different)

I had a lot of free time. I was involved with my friends; playing bowling, tennis and going on short trips with the children. Time was passing and I was busy with the children then we were occupied building our new home and later on with the move. I had lots of parties and involvement with the community. However, never neglected my family duties.

One day in 1988, as my husband and I were sitting watching television when he said to me, "You wanted to continue your education. Are you still interested?" I looked at him and momentarily froze without saying anything. Then I looked again and said, "Yes, I am."

I did not waste any time. I registered immediately at Oakland Community College, Farmington Hills, Michigan. Besides the required English courses, I concentrated on psychology courses. I was committed to learning; nothing would stand in my way now. In two years, I accumulated over 62 credits that I transferred to Oakland University. I began taking courses that were required for a major in psychology. However, I tired of the lab and experiments using rabbits and human subjects and decided to explore an alternative.

I talked to my counselor about my dilemma of how I wanted to become a therapist and not finding the Experimental Psychology Department of value. My guidance counselor suggested that I consider a in Human Resource Development /Guidance Program.

As I was an undergraduate student, during my senior year, as I was in the cafeteria having lunch, one of my teachers, who had taught me several courses, asked me if he could join me. I said no problem. We were talking about my classes and I am about to graduate. Out of the blue one day he asked me saying: "Salma, why do you want to be a psychologist?" I said that I loved the subject and that there is a need for cross-cultural psychologists. He responded with concern saying, "I am afraid that you might get hurt and disappointed and he added that people can be cruel."

At this time I was angry and I asked him, "What do you mean?" He remarked, "You know English is not your first language and people do not like to listen to foreigners with an accent and who are with higher education." It upset me to hear these words because I had been successful in all the courses especially his courses that he taught and maintaining a high grades and better than most of the younger students in the class.

After Lunch I had to go to classes and my internship at the same University. I was disturbed all day with his comment. I always said to myself that I would never let anyone to bring me down to his/her level for any reason. But I was very hurt.

That same day as I was speaking with another instructor/the chair for the Counseling Department who I had also several classes with when he noticed something different in my tone of voice. He asked me: "what is going on, you seem down, maybe I can help you". So I shared with him what had happened with the other instructor. He tried to make excuses for him for me not to feel bad about the situation. I felt better but I did not believe all the excuses.

On the same day after the evening class the female instructor we always with other students left at night together headed toward the parking lot. It was obvious that I was still bothered and I needed more answers. So, I asked the instructor if my accent is bad due to my English as a second language? She said, "Salma, what is wrong? You seem bothered." I told her what had happened. She became angry and had two brief cases in her had which she put down and with a firm voice she said to me, "No! No! Salma no. Don't let anyone discourage you, will. You will make an excellent psychologist. "And she added, "As a matter of fact you have a big plus. You know other languages which will put you ahead of other psychologists."

I believe this instructor was speaking from her heart. However, that comment stayed always on my mind especially in public speaking when I presented special topics wandering how I am being accepted. No matter how much I tried to get over it and tried to continued with my education, his words was always with me.

One thing I was happy when later I learned that the instructor who tried to discourage me was discharged from the university because of several complaints from other students that forced the University to dismiss his employment. I wondered how many students he hurt.

This incident was my first vivid awareness that some people looked at me as a foreigner with an accent, an essential part of my identity. I will never lose these qualities of caring to others and the presence of the inner-voice will not allow others to look down at me because I am an immigrant. I graduated from Oakland University in 1992.

By this time, my husband had accepted the idea of my going to college. He started preparing hot tea for me when I returned home, and eventually, he started making salads and had dinner waiting for me. I want to emphasize that Arab/Chaldean husbands (I mix Arab and Chaldean because we were Chaldeans [Catholic] living in an Arab country) never do these things for their wives. Such behavior is translated into being less than a man. Also, up to this time, I had waited on him, even if he only wanted a glass of water.

I needed to remind myself that I am worthy and responsible for myself. I was feeling down how dared this man try to kill my soul. My self worth was safe with myself and I am worthy to be anything I want. I learned to be prepared for people who try to treat others badly. I learned that no matter how badly people treat me, I would never drop down to their level. Just I know that I am better and walk away.

As soon as I took my first course in the program, I felt mentally charged. The teachings included Rogerian theory and group processes that were congruent with my own values. To my surprise, I had found a link to the study of humanistic psychology.

I started sensing even more changes in him. I approached him about getting a Master's degree, and I had my friend, who was already attending The Center for Humanistic Studies (CHS), in Detroit, describe the intensity and excitement of the program. I wanted my husband to hear about it so that he would understand what I was getting into. I was very pleased that he reaffirmed his support.

I felt aglow with enthusiasm as I work towards my goals. I felt sense of ambitious and determined to achieve my goals. I believe and treasure the values I was brought up with which have added to my sensitivity to the needs of the people around me. My awareness of other people's feelings gave me a feeling of consecutiveness to the world around me.

When I was told that I have to go back and look for a research question, I started the search within myself, trying to unfold and process my thoughts. I had the sense of knowing the answer and yet not being able to pinpoint the exact nature of it. I felt the emptiness but could not get a hand on its source. In my struggle and during the search process, I came across a small book called "Unlocking the Secrets of your Childhood Memories by Dr. Kelvin Leman and Randy Calson. This book propelled me and gave me the guidance to explore my childhood and try to connect that with my adult life.

I treasure my childhood. As I look back, I can say that my childhood was a happy one. I came from a fairly large family and I was one of five brothers and sisters. I rank second oldest, that makes me a middle child. I had nine uncles and aunts who lived on the same block. We lived as one large family, with no boundaries and certainly no family secrets. My parents, uncles, aunts and grand parents gathered every evening. Adults lived their life and children lived theirs. We learned that when the adults gathered there was no room for the children. We were not allowed to sit and listen to the adult conversations.

Innocence is the word that comes to my mind. The children were the pride and the future joy of their families. They were expected to do their best to attain the expectations the parents have set for them. We were brought up secluded from any type of media: there was no television and we were not allowed to listen to the radio and magazines were not brought home. We went to the movies during the Holiday season only.

The only movies that were shown during this period were mostly historical movies. Innocence was prized even through adolescents. Without outside corruption, children could concentrate on being children and mainly on schoolwork. Internalizing those values was important to the individual families' culture.

However, I was different than the rest of the children. I struggled with being outspoken and straightforward with others, which was unacceptable within my culture in a child and certainly not as a girl. Girls were brought up to be sensitive, shy, obedient, and silent. I must have been encouraged to do otherwise because I was not like that at all. I was always asking questions and most of the time I was given no answers because I was told that I was too young.

I was more curious than the rest of the children. I was the strongest of all my brothers, sisters, and cousins. In the games we played I picked up the most important role along with being the leader. The children always followed my decisions. This increased the envy of the children. When challenged I would tell them that I am going to be an important person when I grow up and I deserved these roles.

I believe that my strength came from the adults around me. They had high expectations for me. I was the cutest child and most loved but yet I was not spoiled. I was treated like a princess. Everyone looked up to me and knew that I would be someone special. While I enjoyed the attention I also was anxious that this special treatment would make the other siblings jealous. To neutralize the conflict I developed a strategy of being extremely nice to all and still getting everything my way.

I began to be cautious yet at the same time strengthening my power over my older sister's jealousy, although she was not a threat to me. She had no ambition in life. She took what was given to her and never asked for more. I was completely different I took what was given to me and asked for more. My expectations in life were always very high and I wanted to get the most out of it.

> *Adler (1990) explains:*
> *....the difference between a lady and a flower is not how she behaves, but how she's treated. I shall always be a flower girl to Professor Higgins, because he always treats me as flower girl, and always will; but I know I can be a lady to you, because you always treat me as a lady, and always will. (p. 61)*

My life was full yet there was this feeling of emptiness within myself. I knew I needed something more in my life. I discussed the matter with my husband who tried to discourage me, but I decided to enroll with or without his blessing.

This was the first time I had made a decision on my own and where there was no room for compromise. It was not easy, but being persistent, I decided to make things work. I managed to accommodate my husband and children' needs and at the same time kept my obligation to my decision to do well in school.

I wanted to finish as soon as possible and continue my educational goals at the college level. During lunch I watched the office for more experience and extra credit. Besides the experience, I developed a close relationship with the principal and her assistant.

One day close to the holiday season while busy answering phones in the school office, the principle and her assistant had come back after lunch early and the three of us were in the office. The two of them were in a good mood. Sitting comfortably on the floor, they started telling me how boring life has been for them. Then, they predicted that someday after I would finish my high school, I would attend college and manage to obtain and accomplish a higher educational degree while they would still be at the same school holding the same positions. It seemed that I had stored this information back in my unconscious mind. Processing these memories made me discover the connection somewhere and revealed the prophecy.

> *"Education is the most powerful weapon which you*
> *can use to change the world."*
> *~Nelson Mandela~*

It was not easy going back to school but I had decided to make things work. During this period, I had my first psychology course, which was the trigger for me. I enjoyed the course and I realized that I had a passion for the subject. I found myself staying after class trying to expand my knowledge about the subject. I guess I needed some guidance since the subject was new to me.

During this period, I researched and kept on reading books about psychology.

This led me to comply with my prediction for my future. After some time, I decided that I would pursue my education in psychology. I felt a dynamic awakening of my inner consciousness and realized that I have found the missing link in my life. To be a therapist that is what I was looking for and I was on my way to fulfill my life-long dream. I finished my high school within a two-year period and was ready to go to college.

I had layers and layers of experiences, which I know now, will contribute to my success. Like a rose, each action represented a petal to add and I became a whole new me. I now was on the path to understanding and giving meaning to my prophecy. Within the last couple of years, I have felt like a bird soaring higher and higher with new areas of knowledge. A whole new world has opened for me where there are no limits except those that I impose on myself.

After graduating from Oakland University and looking back I wondered why my husband changed his mind and agreed for me to continue college. Whether he wanted me off his back, since I constantly reminded him all the time that he has spoiled my opportunities in life, or maybe he wanted me to use my time wisely and I was truly interested in completing my education plans. I cannot believe how much he has changed. Our relationship has grown spontaneously. I was always told that if we change others around us would change.

Now I realize the depth and love we feel for each other. I can feel his support for me besides being proud of me too. Moreover, my husband helps with the house chores and preparing meals, which left me full of appreciation. This is not an easy role for my husband since men in the Iraqi culture do not help women with house chores. I certainly applaud my husband for, without his help and support, I could have not been able to fulfill my dreams.

When I wake up every morning, on my way to the Center for Humanistic Studies the excitement leads me to the knowledge of power and a feeling of wholeness. Now for the first time I am in a peaceful mode remembering my experiences and the depth of meaning life has for me now. Sometimes I do not believe what has happened to me. I find myself thinking if this is one of my dreams and then I feel an overwhelming excitement and peace within myself and realize it is not. There was certainly intentional self-research in looking for a way to fulfill my self-prophecy. The awareness grew until I could no longer put off investigating it.

In this section I did uncover the experiences that made me express my anger and tension helping me to see the world more clearly. It is clear that I have traced some of the moments when things came together for me. My experiences have converged into a conscious desire to learn more about my prophecy when everything will come together.

I started with my own experience that will lead the way to understand how others felt about the facts of the topic. This was to help me expand my research and bring to the surface the questions and answers. My hope was to explore with others the experience of a self-fulfilling prophecy. I wanted to contribute my knowledge and understanding to others and reach new dimensions in understanding. I believe that others will also benefit from my investigation.

In the preparation of the research that had been a dynamic process, and my involvement in it has changed me significantly. I am very curious to find out if other people have had the same experience of prophecy as I have. I wonder if others found themselves conforming to external cues or internal, listening to themselves or others.

Finally, I was able to know that people find self-fulfilling prophecy as positive self-trusting at the end of their experience. I planed to search these wanderings by asking the question: "What is the Experience of Self-fulfilling Prophecy?"

I discovered myself as I was exploring issues and experiences in my life related to my Master Thesis with the question, "What is the Experience of a Self-fulfilling Prophecy?"

I am aware that this quest is the mystery hidden within me and is waiting to be self discovered. While waiting to enter the Master's program at the Center for Humanistic Studies, memories of my past began sweeping my mind.

I know the answer is within me connected with my past all I need to do is collect my thoughts. It has been a long journey and will continue, as I realize my own internal needs. There was a struggle within myself with the emptiness I have always felt inside me. I was always aware of my search for answers that would satisfy the empty feelings I experienced.

In the early stages of my marriage, I shared these feelings of emptiness with my husband and he always managed to convince me that my happiness should only include him and the children. I believed in my husband and yet I believed in myself and knew I needed to fill the emptiness. I realized this emptiness had to do with a dream I have of getting an education at a higher level. Why then am I giving in and not fighting for myself? I knew I was capable of doing just that and I have the strong personality to accomplish my goals.

Most of the results and findings were positive and "they were responsible for their lives and will take only the positives and do not wait too long to make the change

Without it I could not have completed my Master's Degree in Clinical Psychology and an advanced Specialist Degree in the same field. He is even more supportive and proud of me when I enrolled in a Ph.D. program at The Union Institute. I believe that our relationship become increasingly closer and our understanding of each other's needs has grown strong because of the sharing that was made possible by his support of my studies. This was also made a big cultural impact upon our close friends and relatives.

As I finalize many of the learning opportunities of my Ph.D. program, at The Union Institute, I found myself becoming more focused as a person and more qualified as a professional. I am aware that most of the time I push the limits of my potential and became increasingly competent and effective. I was aware of the interpersonal changes and to my surprise my husband has grown and changed too.

When I began working with the Arab Community for Economic and Social Services (ACCESS), as the coordinator and supervisor for the Developmental Disability Program, I did not know what challenges I would face.

I have enjoyed putting my learning into practice. I developed my own assessments of Arabic speaking clients, provided psychological testing, and engaged in psychotherapy with families. Although this job was demanding, I learned that I could work effectively with many different populations. I realized again and again that people are resourceful human beings.

Chapter 28

Personal Knowledge in following my dream

> *The self- concept is such a powerful force on the*
> *personality that it not only determines how you see*
> *yourself in the present but also can actually influence*
> *your future behavior and that of others. Such occurrence*
> *comes about through a phenomenon called the self-*
> *fulfilling prophecy.*
> *(Adler, 1990. p. 64)*

Personal Knowledge and Experience

Today, looking back on my life, which is full of meanings and with my profound thoughts deep inside; "I wouldn't want change a thing". I believe it was a blessing. All the experiences I had made me the person I am today. It made me stronger and better person. As I examined throughout my experiences I came to discover the logical thinking that I always been known for among my family and friends allowed me to be always ahead of time.

There is a power within me that guides me on a path that I have designed. Suddenly things begin to fall into place. I feel strong I do not get discouraged when I am challenged. I do not mind losing friends who are inpatient with me when I grant my studies and research priority. Higher Education is my goal. I am determined to succeed in obtaining the doctoral degree.

My research interest was powerfully influenced by my interaction with immigrants and refugees. Some chose the United States as an alternative and permanent home; others, (e.g. the refugees) had no choice in-to which country they would land. Over the past 20 years, I have found myself comforting these individuals and helping them in many ways, guiding and empowering them to be able to gain control over their own lives.

As a humanistic psychologist, I have recognized throughout this research the value of descriptions of experience from the individual person's internal frame of reference. I chose to investigate the experience of being an immigrant because it offered opportunities to contribute to cultural diversity.

Right then at that moment, I have felt a change beginning to happen. The change that has come from within, guided by an inner wisdom that has propelled me to achieve my goals. Back then, at last, I have experienced a new depth of peace, faith, love, and success in the process of reaching my goals. Just like the seasons, people have the ability to change.

With my commitment and faith and, I found out that my inner self have guided me to overcome the challenges to reach my dreams by transforming myself. I felt a spiritual awakening and I was clear about my intentions. I will never allow anyone to take me away from my passion is in my hand and my sacred self is I am worthy.

During my contact with immigrants and their families it became clear to me that they suffer from multiple stressors including language barriers, lack of language skills, resources, lack of transportation and financial difficulties. At first, I thought their stories were exaggerated, but when I started listening to one after another relating their experience of the immigration process, I decided to research the topic.

People move to this country in search of prosperity, equality, freedom, and financial success. The immigrant leaves his or her mother country, ordinarily by legal means, and chooses to live here in America as a citizen wanting desperately to call this new place home.

I believe that my journey of discovery of the meaning of the immigration experience, is the paradigm of the moment when the experience is real, all at once, its essence, its profound meanings are universal and personal.

In my research, I have attempted to capture an understanding of the actual experience of the immigrant. I have attempted to discover, distinctive meanings, prevailing themes, and intrinsic aspects of the process of immigration. The experience has been described in texts in sociology and psychology and in fiction, autobiography and drama. I believe that I have arrived at some new understandings and knowledge of the experience of being an immigrant.

The United States is known as the nation of immigrants. Hundreds of thousands of people have come together here from every corner of the Universe. Many leave their home country each year driven by poverty, persecution or the hope of a better life. Most of these individuals seek a permanent visa; some seek political asylum; others are refuge seekers, forced out of their homeland by war, natural disasters and persecution.

So who are these people? Where do they come from? What are their cultural and religious beliefs? What is the full range of their experience and dreams? My research was designed to review social and cultural differences and to explicate the experience of immigrants. In this process, I have been welcomed into broken hearts and broken homes; have lived with my co-researchers in their descriptions of interrupted lives, separated families, known and frightening surroundings, social displacements, racism, and traumatic experiences.

I have come to a comprehensive understanding of the meaning of the experience of being an immigrant and have come to terms with my own life, and have discovered insights into other's experiences.

While immigration involves a process, portrayal of the experience may help newcomers upon arrival. In my experience I searched for my own identity. In Iraq, where I grew up, children and women had no identity. I was constantly questioning why I should do this or that. That was exactly what was on my mind when I immigrated to the United States, so I made a firm decision to claim the freedom I had always longed for evoking feelings that Moustakas (1995) describes so well:

> *...Being free means being at home with one-self, willing to disclose to one's own immediate feelings and thoughts, moods, and internal states....Freedom is a yardstick through which attachment is enhanced; it is the source of new energy and validity; it is a way of being that enables us to feel just right about ourselves and others. (p. 92)*

As I was growing up, I had my own thinking. I asked lots of questions but there were many things I was not allowed to speak about. After I married, my husband affirmed my right to freedom to think and to choose to do what would make me happy. He also believed in freedom of the mind. Making life decisions requires freedom of mind. Sheehy (1981) discloses other facets of the experience:

Change always involves loss. Part of the experience of the separation phase is, of necessity, some degree of anxiety and depression. Mixed with frightening and mournful moods is often an innocent, springing joy: a lightening, a washing away of the caked mud of compromise. The alteration of those moods is what gives this phase its bittersweet quality, like the swing of moods in early adolescence. (p. 74)

In reviewing the literature, I found a little booklet, I was dreaming to come to America: Memories from the Ellis Island Oral History Project. In this, Giuliani (1997) who is the mayor of New York City draws the reader's attention to memories and experiences of the 12 million European immigrants who came through Ellis Island. This book was meant for children of immigrants to help them find their own family stories. A newly arrived 19 year old from Italy, in 1914, said:

> *When I got here at Ellis Island, for three days on that island. I slept there, I ate there for three days....But for that time, [it]was awfully bad. Scary. Because you don't have no mother no more, you've taken off from the mother and father. You're travelling on your own. I mean, you leave your mother, you cry...for your mother all the time, so I wrote a letter to my mother from the Ellis Island. Told my mother that I got off, I got a job. And it made my mother strong. (Giuliani, 1997, p.36)*

The Iraq-Iran war, followed by the Gulf-war, left many Iraqi's no choice but to leave the country. The U.S. was preferred because relatives resided there.

My entire program of study has prepared me to make a significant contribution to helping individuals and families newly arrived to this country in terms of adjustments, residence, and vocation. Through my studies of humanistic and clinical psychology, I have learned how to facilitate change and provide guidance.

Chapter 29

Healing with the Angels

"*Wherever you go*

Whatever you do

May your Guardian Angel

Watch over you"

A baby is an angel whose wings decrease as his legs increase. ~Author Unknown~

My Guardian angel

I have many questions about my guardian angel and his job. At this point in my journey, rather than becoming discouraged or running off to many other sources, it would be best to place myself close to my guardian angel and listen to.

When I registered for the psychology class for my high school Diploma, I began watching things around me that I have never done before. I began using my psychology learning into practice. In reading stories regarding incidents that people had experienced in their lives.

In my first Psychology class the teacher brought a speaker to the class introduced her as a "Psychic" let's call her Laura. Laura introduced her self and she asked all students to form a circle. She started asking questions. The first student Laura questioned about her family and where they lived and that she can see someone is hanging in a rope. The girl was surprised and confirmed the psychic's insight that hanging man was her great grandfather who was hung during the civil war in the south.

Laura asked the next student about the family and the psychic started describing a lady she can see someone in the kitchen baking breads. The student confirmed that she grew up around her grand mother who used to bake bread every day.

Then comes my turn Laura looked at me and she asked me if I had a baby sister or a brother that died when I was a baby. I was speechless when Laura said to me that she could see a baby crawling around my bed. She added that this is my guardian angel that has saved me from several dangerous incidents. I was unable to comment and said to Laura to pass.

That same night went to my bed to sleep as usual I jumped on my bed. Immediately I thought about Laura "she was right" I thought to myself. I have been doing this all my life would jump on the bed feeling there was a baby and I was afraid to step on it. I had the chills that night and I was afraid to mention that to my husband fearing that he will make fun of it and will say to me that I am going crazy.

I kept these feelings to myself. Years ago after that my son brought a baby cat home. I did not want to stay but he insisted that the cat to stay. So I agreed that the cat to stay. After few months one night I was sleeping in my and usually I lock my bedroom door when my husband is out until he comes home. As I was lying down covered with the comforter I felt that there was a movement on the comforter. With fear I lifted my head and I saw the movement on my bed. Immediately I made the sign of the cross on my face and froze. I was dead scared waiting for my husband to come.

While we are sleeping, angels have conversations with our souls.
~Author Unknown ~

The following days I was thinking about that incident. I am used to attend a woman Spiritual Retreat. I called and registered to attend. During the retreat I approached the Retreat Director about the incident and I have a lot of fear. Her answer to me was to speak to my baby sister and not to be afraid. The director who is a nun she said to me to reflect on past event with potentially serious consequences that I might be able to remember that my guardian angle has saved me.

Jack's Winning Words 7/15/13
"The most incredible thing about miracles is that they happen." (G.K. Chesterton) Most of us can identify with "Doubting" Thomas, wanting proof before we believe in a miracle (something that seems to go against the laws of nature). A miracle can also be an ordinary event that shows the presence of God, an indicator that He is in our life. They happen all the time, and we often take them for granted. Watch for one today! ;-) Jack

I can recall several incidents that I was protected. I remember when I was 4 years old I was in Kindergarten when we were to take the bus home. I said to my sister to stop the bus I had to go to the bathroom. I come out the bus and my sister was gone and I was alone in the school. I sat there crying. It started to get dark and I was even more afraid and more crying and there was no one to hear me. Finally later on the bus came back with my father and the bus driver and picked me up.

I believe that my Guardian Angel shield me with his wings. This was the other incident happened to me on my 5th birthday as I stated earlier when my sister pushed me down the stairs. Those stairs were built out of concrete to fall about 18 steps down with a minor bleeding.

The other incident was in Kuwait that I have talked about in earlier chapter. It seemed that my guardian angel was again to protect me and shield me from danger.

Another very scary incident I have not discussed in this book earlier. Being in the States for about five years. My husband always encouraged me to take the children in summer vacation since he is working alone in the business and cannot leave.

I decided to go to California and visit the entire state. The plan was to make the first step in Turlock California where my aunt lived there. I took her with me as a companion only and help me with the children. Mind you she did not speak English and she had no clue how to act in an emergencies). The plan worked well. We travelled by gray Hound bus from one city to other. We started by visiting Lake Tahoe we stayed 3 days we stayed in the Casino and had great time.

Our next stop was San Francisco where we stayed in a nice hotel by the ocean.

San Francisco had a great system for busses and we were using the buses since I was new in this country to rent a car not knowing the road with 3 (ages 3, 7,9) children. Inside the state of California was safer to travel by bus.

> *Your Guardian Angel knows you inside and out, and*
> *loves you just the way you are!*
> **~Author Unknown ~**

We decided to visit the Chinese Tea Garden that we enjoyed. We left the Chinese Garden where there was a bus stop. I did not know the bus number that takes us to visit China Town. While waiting for the bus I told my aunt to stay with the children for me to go to the gas station to use the public phone to check on the number of the bus that will take us to China Town.

When I got to the gas station there was no pay phone. Returning to the bus stop, I saw a building with the door open, a woman sitting by the desk with a phone in front of her. As naive as I was I asked the lady if I could use the phone. She looked at the stairs as another lady coming down the stars she answered yes she can use the pay phone.

One of these women called the guy who was very big, tall and chunky. He said to me come I will show you the pay phone so I walked behind him where we entered the first room I say young guys laying on bare floor followed the man to the next room there was more young girls laying on the bare floor. Immediately I became scared and panicking I made the sign of the cross on my side waist and I said God help me. It was like someone held me by my shoulders and turned me toward the front door. I just wanted to see the road out of the house hearing the man's voice after me telling me that the phone is here. All I wanted to get out.

Finally I joined my aunt and my children hugging them all. My aunt looked concerned and she asked me what happened to you; it seems you have just seen a ghost? I said to her I would tell you later. A Bus stopped and I asked the driver what is number of the bus that we can take to China Town? He gave me the correct bus number for us to take. The other bus came after very shortly and we took it to China Town. We went through it quick and I said to my aunt I want to visit a church before we go to the hotel. She agreed.

There was a church close by and we went in and asked to talk to a priest. A priest came and sat with us in a room. I started telling him about the incident at that house by the Chinese Tea Garden. The priest said to me you were lucky that you were out in time. He continued informing us that hundreds of young people vanish out of sight on a daily basis and are being sold and used for slave/sex trafficking and no one would ever find them again. He added to me that my guardian's angel is the one that turned me toward the door forcing me to leave.

Chapter 30

How great it is living in America

"Remember, remember always, that all of us, and you and I especially, are descended from immigrants and revolutionists."
-Franklin D. Roosevelt-

As I come toward the final chapters, there are so much to say to my grand children about "The Iraq I used to know" that I wished that I had the chance to take them back to see what a great country it was. Iraq was the best country in the Middle East with its location and its people. However, we made the right choice in moving to the United States of America when we felt the change approaching our mother country.

As I keep emphasized earlier that we made the right choice for us and our children and future grandchildren to live in piece. We adopted our new life and everything we were able to transform ourselves. I feel blessed and appreciate my background and the good times and traditions will never be forgotten, and want to share with my children and all the children of the Iraqi immigrants who might never have the chance to know where they came from, and this is part of the American culture.

At the present time

As I come to almost the last chapter, there are so much to say to my grand children about the "Iraq I used to know" that I wished that

I had the chance to take them back to see what a great country it was. Iraq was the best country in the Middle East with its location and its people. However, we made the right choice in moving to the states when we felt the change approaching the country.

As I keep emphasized earlier that we made the right choice for us and our children and future grandchildren to live in piece. We adopted our new life as we acculturated into the American Culture, as we were ready for the change. Everything became normal to us, and our good times and traditions will never be forgotten, and this is part of the American Dream. We were able to make ourselves feel better by making major changes within our family and ourselves.

Part of restoring the culture I was able to keep the children close to home and grow with both cultures to be proud who they were before coming the United States and who thy are now. We allowed them to make healthy choices and encouraged them to get their education to have the power to be responsible for their lives and their children to come.

When we built our second home, it was our dream home and we still live in. Our desire was to keep our children close to us, living in the same area. We bought three properties for the three children in the same subdivision. I wanted to keep the children and the grand children close to us and not lose them.

The children knew that their friends are welcomed to come to our home to sleep over or after school when they know that I have cooked their favorite food like stuffed grape leaves with lamb meat and rice with our traditional spices. My children's friends seemed that they smell the good home cooking and they come to my home after school to eat their favorite meal.

We kept the children in Catholic schools and they did well. I wanted them to attend Catholic schools because I wanted them to have what we had in Iraq my husband and me. Where I attended all girls French nuns school in Basra, and their dad attended all boys American Jesuit's school in Baghdad. The two oldest ones were OK with all boys school, however their younger brother his high school was also boys only Catholic school. After two years he wanted to transfer to a public school because these schools have mixed boys and girls.

As the boys started growing up their dad took them to help him with the business during the summer vacation. I did not mind to keep them busy. I also took them on trips and we enjoyed the summer vacation together since their dad was not able to leave the business.

We took advantage of long weekends to travel all of us as a family and the children enjoyed their dad being with them. We gave them love and we did not have any preferred one over the others. We treated them all the same. We wanted them to love each other as well.

We tried to speak with them in English as well as Arabic, however since they conversed with each other in English that seemed to be easier for them. As they stated getting older they seemed to trying to speak in Arabic. The three of them can understand the Arabic Language and can speak it somehow. Now since my oldest son's wife speak fluent Arabic and Chaldean. The youngest son who is engaged and his fiancé speaks Chaldean only so he wants to learn the Chaldean Language and I have encouraged him to do so.

We managed to keep the boys around us by purchasing for them property when they were young. The plan was for them to stay close by in the same subdivision. The oldest two built their homes in the same subdivision we live at. The youngest son lives about four miles away from us. The boys and the grandchildren visit us almost on daily basis.

Sundays has been a tradition We attend the early morning Mass so that we can prepare breakfast for the children to come after church all come for breakfast where my husband and I prepare breakfast to eat together and the grandchildren love it. This way we try to keep them close and their children will teach their own children about the culture and the important that they keep close together.

During breakfast we usually discuss what has happened in the community and our extended Family. While we have breakfast they hear about our week and we discuss their own. The children are interested to hear what is going on with our family. The grandchildren enjoy Papa's Omelet and potatoes fruits and cheese.

Chapter 31

"If you choose to place your happiness on external factors, you will be constantly searching for that next "want." Yet, if you place your happiness on what lives inside of you, you'll be able to find contentment and peace of mind."

Michelle Sedas, Inspired Living Center

Today:

The Immigrants American Dream

Now I come to the last chapter, I dedicate this book to my children, grandchildren and the Iraqi children who will never have my experience growing up in Iraq. There is so much to say to my grand children about the "Iraq I know" I wish that I had the chance to take them back to see what a great country it was. Iraq was the best country in the Middle East, with its location and its people. However, we made the right choice in moving to the states when we felt the changes approaching our country in a negative way.

We raised our children to think about the American Dream that made thousands of families leave their own country and follow their dream. They grew up realizing that we made the sacrifice to come for a better future for them. They truly appreciate being Americans, to enjoy the freedom.

We made the right choice for us and our children and future grandchildren to live in peace. We adopted our new life and everything became normal and benefit having the good times and traditions will never be forgotten, and this is part of the American culture.

I always remind my children that we love Iraq as our mother country, and at the same time we love America more. We made the choice to leave Iraq and adopt the United States as our permanent country, to raise our children in a healthy environment. We always discussed our culture is important that we keep it and pass it on to our children, and for them to pass it to their own children

As the years go by, we always reminded our children that we were an excellent example for them that we assimilated with the American culture, and at the same time we were proud to keep our own culture as a reminder to them to appreciate where they came from. Within time they accepted both cultures and loving both equally.

I have known individuals (men and women) who are stuck within their cultures and traditions, trying very hard not to becoming part of the American culture. Their will to become part of this new country is very slim and mix into the culture is very difficult to try to change. They refuse to go to schools that teach English as a second Language. This was the scenario when we came to the States 40 years ago.

Today, arriving new Iraqi Refugees are more educated with the English Language, technology and computers. We find some are very eager to find a job or taking classes to improve their language. Others are stuck and feel sorry for them selves finding others, friends and relatives who came before them are well established doing well and they want to be in their level. They are working harder to make ends meet.

Others find themselves relying on the American Government or their relatives in order to meet their needs. We make choices in life, and these choices draw for us our path that will lead us to our future.

I have heard from American Born people who are not satisfied with their lives and would rather be in another country. I always challenge them that living in the United States is the right place to be. You will never know how good you have it until you visit other countries. We have so many advantages living and working in America and most of is security and freedom of speech and religion.

Some people get into America to live with their family members who are residing in the country. Equally, a person who gets a Green

Card in America or becomes a US citizen can sponsor other relatives and bring them to America. Immigration can be easy through a fiancé's visa that ends with marriage, and also permits them to experience the good life the country offers. Moreover, people in America are creative and the cultural and racial diversity are two important factors that make people love the country.

Many hate to live in countries with no international influences and such people choose to get into America as the country that has people from various places and different cultures. Likewise, people in America can write and speak about anything they wish and they may not be penalized for doing so. But this may not be possible in many other foreign countries and people in other countries cannot dare to speak against the government; They may be assassinated or put in jail by the governments. These are a few best things about the United States that draws the attention of almost all the foreign nationals.

A new addition to the family

My oldest son Faris was married to Asil (15) years ago. I was happy to have Asil as a daughter since I had only 3 boys and always wanted a daughter. We were blessed with two grandchildren, Christian (14) and Grace (12). They live across the street from us and we see them everyday when they come over. The grandchildren love to sleep over at our house as we watch TV together, and they make popcorn while we watch movies of their choice. The next morning, I make them breakfast of their choice with tea. These are a few traditions we enjoy together. Christmas time we make Christmas cookies at Easter we color the eggs together. The grandchildren love to drink tea with Nana and they call it chai chai.

Final note: Shennel is my youngest son Ramzi Jr's wife. They were married on May 31, 2014. She is a very energetic, sweet young lady, and is such a wonderful addition to our family. I would like to share a note I wrote for Shennel on her wedding day.

I would like to welcome you, Shennel, into our family. I wanted to tell you on this day how much you mean to me. Our family is so very blessed to have gained someone as beautiful as you. I have seen the kindness in your heart, and the special way you loved my son. I am proud of you for the happiness you brought into his life and I know deep in my heart he is joyful to have gained such a loving wife.

- Finally, my husband and I are delighted on the arrival of our third grandchild, Hailey Rose, on April 25, 2015. She is the firstborn of my youngest son, Ramzi Jr. and his lovely wife Shennel.

Printed in the United States
By Bookmasters